WORSHIPING IN THE WILDERNESS

Vertical Worship ♦ A Personal Look

ANGELA D. BROWN

*"O God of my life, I'm lovesick for You in this weary wilderness.
I thirst with the deepest longings to love You more,
with cravings in my heart that can't be described.
Such yearning grips my soul for You, my God!"*

Psalms 63:1 [The Passion Translation]

Copyrights

All rights reserved. No part of this publication may be reproduced, stored in a retrieval system or transmitted in any form by any means, electronic, mechanical, photocopy, recording or otherwise, without the prior permission of the publisher.

For information contact:
Vertical Worship Ministries
1050 Oaklane Drive
Orangeburg, SC 29115
ISBN: 978-1-0882-8294-6

All scripture quotations unless otherwise indicated are taken from the Holy Bible King James Version

Scripture quotations marked from NKJV are taken from the New King James Version copyrighted © 1982 by Thomas Nelson Inc. Used by permission. All rights reserved.

Scripture quotations marked NIV are from the International Bible Society copyrighted in June 1978. Published by Broadman & Holman

Scripture quotations marked TPT are from The Passion Translation copyrighted in 2020 Passion & Fire Ministries, Inc. Published by Broadstreet Publishing Group, LLC

Scripture quotations marked HCSB have been taken from the Holman Christian Standard Bible ® Copyright © 1999, 2000, 2002, 2003, 2009 by Holman Bible Publishers. Used by Permission Holman Christian Standard Bible ® Holman CSB ®

Table of Contents

INTRODUCTION --- 4

Is it Hot in Here or Am I Just Thirsty? ---------------------- 12

Did I Backslide? --- 20

What Season Is It? --- 26

My Beginning --- 29

The Great Epiphany (The Original One) ------------------------ 32

A Change in Religion --- 35

New Beginnings --- 38

Dancing for the King --- 41

Vertical Worship – The Principles ---------------------------- 43

Is My worship Really Vertical? ------------------------------- 45

Worshiping in The Wilderness - It's My Turn Now -------------- 47

How I Worship Vertically in the Wilderness ------------------- 49

   Principle #1 - Knowing God ---------------------------------- 53

   Principle #2 - Die to Self ---------------------------------- 58

   Principle #3 - Practice His Presence ------------------------ 65

   Principle #4 - Acknowledge the Personage of the Holy Spirit - 71

   Principle #5 - Acknowledge His Deity [Lordship] -------------- 78

   Principle #6 - Tell Him You Love Him often ------------------- 83

Principle #7 - Sing Love Songs to Him ---------------------------- *90*

Principle #8 - Develop a Lasting Friendship with Him --------- *94*

Principle #9 - Don't Isolate Yourself ------------------------------ *97*

Principle #10 - Bathe Yourself in the Word of God ------------- *102*

Principle #11 - Exercise – Start Moving! ------------------------ *110*

Principle #12 - PRAY! Talk to God ------------------------------ *113*

Worshiping Through a Pandemic ----------------------------------- **119**

Worshiping through Sickness ------------------------------------- **127**

Worshiping Through Grief -- **132**

Coming Out of the Fog…I Choose Christ ------------------------ **137**

The Benefits of Worshiping in the Wilderness ------------------ **147**

I Promise You -- **152**

Let My Life Be Worship -- **155**

REFERENCES --- **157**

Dedication

This book is dedicated to all those who love the Lord but struggle to maintain a consistent relationship with Him during the difficult times of life. I pray that this book gives you the determination to rekindle that passionate love relationship with the Lord.

And for those who do not know the Lord, may it kindle a passion to get to know Him even in the midst of pressing life circumstances.

Whatever stage of life you may find yourself in at this moment in time, remember that He is Jehovah Shammah – The Lord is There.

A Personal Conviction Disclaimer

I have a personal reverence for the Lord which will stand out in this book. Whenever I am writing about the Lord, out of profound respect, I capitalize the pronouns when referring to God, Jesus or the Holy Spirit (even in the scriptural reference). So even though it may be grammatically incorrect, you will see throughout all my writings the capitalization of the following words: He, Him, His, My, Mine, You, and Yours.

Worshiping in the Wilderness

Psalm 63:1-8
The Passion Translation (TPT)

"O God of my life, I'm lovesick for You in this weary wilderness.
I thirst with the deepest longings to love You more,
with cravings in my heart that can't be described.
Such yearning grips my soul for You, my God!
I'm energized every time I enter
Your heavenly sanctuary to seek more of Your power
and drink in more of Your glory.
For Your tender mercies mean more to me than life itself.
How I love and praise You, God!
Daily I will worship You passionately and with all my heart.
My arms will wave to You like banners of praise.
I overflow with praise when I come before You,
for the anointing of Your presence satisfies me like nothing else.
You are such a rich banquet of pleasure to my soul.
I lie awake each night thinking of You
and reflecting on how You help me like a father.
I sing through the night under Your splendor-shadow,
offering up to You my songs of delight and joy!
With passion I pursue and cling to You.
Because I feel Your grip on my life,
I keep my soul close to Your heart."

INTRODUCTION

Human relationships have seasons. Sometimes they are very close and sometimes they are distant. Sometimes they share happy events and other times they share sad events. No matter what season you are in, if that relationship has any value to you, you must protect it at all costs.

I was fortunate enough to witness my parents celebrate over 50 years of marriage, and like most relationships, they experienced ups and downs. They had disagreements and arguments, but because of their love and commitment to each other, they remained together until my mother went home to be with the Lord in 2012. Their relationship served as my first example of what a real relationship between a man and woman should look like. Their commitment taught me how to love during good times and bad, and how to commit to the end. Over the years, I have often found myself thanking God for giving me parents who stayed together "till death do us part." Because of them, I learned the art of commitment and incorporated this necessary principle in other relationships in my life, including my friends, my work, and my church. But the most important relationship in which I learned how to commit is the one with my Lord and Savior Jesus Christ.

Over 40 years ago, I accepted Jesus Christ into my life. I not only accepted Him as my personal Savior, but I also accepted Him as a friend, and I wanted more. I wanted to be with Him all the time. I wanted to get to know Him. I wanted to know what brought Him joy and what brought Him sorrow. I learned later that what I wanted was a personal relationship with God.

Having a relationship with God is different from the act of salvation. Once you accept Christ into your life, you are then saved from death, hell, and destruction, but after salvation comes relationship, and after relationship is developed, then intimacy is formed. I wanted more than salvation, so I pursued God. I talked to Him constantly, and I spent time with Him. I shared my heart with Him, and the end product was a personal and intimate relationship with Jesus Christ. And like my parents, sometimes the relationship was on fire and I was in passionate pursuit of Him and there were other times when I was disappointed and stopped talking to Him. But even when I was feeling the most disconnected from the Lord, I knew He was always still there, and that I wasn't going anywhere. Because, when I accepted Jesus Christ into my heart, I not only accepted Him as my Lord and Savior, but I also entered into a committed relationship with Him.

Early in my walk with the Lord, I remember my assistant pastor asking a very important question over the pulpit. He asked, "Are you _enjoying_ life or are you _enduring_ it?" I found this question so profound that I still use it as a measure of where I am in relationship with God today. There are times when I could say that I was truly enjoying life, but there are other times, when I can honestly admit that I was merely enduring life. I look at those times when I was "merely enduring life" as my wilderness experiences. I was dry, barely existing, and I didn't sense the closeness to my Friend, the Savior of my soul, like I once did. It was my ability to worship vertically during those wilderness experiences that has kept me sane.

Before I continue, I want to take some time to share with you what I mean when I mention the term "worship vertically." The idea was originally birthed from a theme for the International Creative Arts Conference I hosted in 2008. When the Lord first gave me the conference theme of Vertical Worship, I was excited. First, He gave me the scripture Colossians 3:1-4; *"If ye then be risen with Christ, seek those things which are above, where Christ sitteth on the right hand of God. Set your affection on things above, not on things on the earth. For ye are dead, and your life is hid with Christ in God."* So immediately I knew it had something to do with my relationship with Christ.

Next, He gave me a logo. I saw the words **Vertical Worship** on a cross. "Vertical" was written on the vertical beam, which would have an arrow pointing upward to show how it was reaching toward heaven indefinitely. The horizontal beam had the word "worship," representing our adoration to the One who died on the cross for our sins.

And that's when the concept hit me. *"Before we can minister to the world horizontally, we must first worship the Lord vertically,"* thus the term "Vertical Worship" was born. In other words, I must first establish a relationship with the Lord by nourishing it and keeping it as my number one priority, then I can truly minister to

Him from a place of love and reverence. It's only then that I can effectively minister to the world.

I took this newfound theme and ran with it. I had the words "Vertical Worship" printed on bags, T-shirts and pens. I was excited to reveal this concept to everyone. Unfortunately, once the conference began and I asked the registrants, "How many of you know what Vertical Worship means?" I was met with blank stares. Nobody knew what it meant. It was because of this that the Lord led me to write my first book entitled *Vertical Worship - What It Is and How to Do It*.

I have observed in life that people worship many different things. Over centuries, mankind has worshiped everything from the sun, animals, and all types of inanimate objects to their favorite movie stars, athletes, and leaders. Unfortunately, the Lord has not always been the object of their worship. The concept behind Vertical Worship is to keep Jesus Christ as our chief focal point. Vertical Worship says, "No one else in this world is as important to me as You are, Lord, and I want to spend my life seeking You, loving You, and fixing my gaze on You." Vertical Worship says, "I will only find true contentment and purpose in life by keeping God first and everything else second. And once that personal relationship with the Lord has been solidified, then I can truly be effective in ministering to the world and winning souls for Christ."

In my pursuit of worshiping God vertically, He originally gave me eight practical principles to incorporate in my daily life. These principles include knowing God, dying to self, telling Him that you love Him, singing love songs to Him, maintaining a friendship with God, and acknowledging the Holy Spirit and His Deity. I will be sharing each of these principles in greater detail later in this book.

Vertical Worship was never meant to be a catchy phrase or cliché. No, it means so much more than that. Vertical Worship is a change in our mindsets.

In this book, I will share very intimately what Vertical Worship means to me. I will share how the Lord revealed the concept of Vertical Worship to me and how I practice it on a daily basis. I also want to share with you how I used Vertical Worship while I was going through my own wilderness experiences for you may experience several throughout your lifetime. I believe that we can still maintain a relationship with God even in our driest seasons. I believe that worshiping God is an intentional act of love. At times it is sacrificial, but whether it's intentional or sacrificial, I believe that worshiping God is a matter of the heart.

Even during my darkest times in the wilderness, my love for God never wavered. Even when I wasn't studying the Word, praying fervently, or laying down my plate, I never stopped communicating with God because I knew that He loved me and I loved Him. We were just going through a dry season. The strong foundation that I laid during my passionate seasons with God carried me through those dry seasons in the wilderness.

I'm going back to the beginning to share how I navigated through my own wilderness experience. Thank you for coming on this journey with me.

DEFINITIONS

As a writer, I love using words and I love looking up the definitions of words, especially new words. That being said, I will be using definitions throughout the book at the beginning of each chapter just to give you a little more clarity or insight into what I am about to share with you. Most definitions are taken from Merriam-webster.com, the Easton Bible Dictionary or the Google dictionary.

Let's start by defining some key words that I will be using throughout this book:

wil·der·ness: noun - an uncultivated, uninhabited, and **inhospitable region**. A neglected or abandoned area of a garden or town; unfriendly. Lacking a favorable climate.

dry season: any season in which little rain falls.

drought/drout: noun- a prolonged period of abnormally low rainfall, leading to a shortage of water.

I will be using the terms "dry season" and "wilderness" interchangeably throughout this book to describe periods of aloneness, or the sense of feeling far away from God that we all experience at one time or another as Christians.

*"The wilderness is **full of loneliness, self-doubt, questioning, and despair**. We feel knocked down and terribly alone."*

Pastor Jay Robison

Is it Hot in Here or Am I Just Thirsty?

*"My soul **thirsts**, pants, and longs for the living God. I want to come and see the face of God."*
Psalm 42:2 [KJV]

Definition: **thirsty** - feeling thirst, deficient in moisture, having a strong desire for something.

Imagine that you are in the wilderness. From what I've seen on TV, it's an unfamiliar place. It's a dry place without the conveniences of home. It's a place where wild animals roam, food is scarce, and there is no one in sight for miles. For the purposes of this book, when I speak of being in the wilderness, I will be looking at it from a spiritual point of view, but before I get there, I want to give you a few definitions of what a wilderness is. Meridian dictionary describes the **wilderness** as "an uncultivated, uninhabited, and inhospitable region; unfriendly." The Hebrew word for wilderness is *midbar*, a land or a climate having little or no rain; too dry or barren to support vegetation. A place where crops cannot grow. The Greek word for wilderness is *eremos*, which means "a sense of aloneness, or solitary." So to summarize, the wilderness is a place that is uninhabited, dry, does not support growth, and is a place of aloneness.

Another word that I like to use for wilderness is "dry season." In the tropics, ***dry seasons*** are described as the lack of water and food supply, and at times, it can coincide with the rise of certain diseases.

According to Wikipedia.org, "a *dry season* is characterized by its low humidity and some watering holes and rivers drying up and can last up to eight months." In a dry season, the lack of water for a period of time is defined as a ***drought.***

Now, let's look at the spiritual definition of the wilderness. According to Holmes Rolston of the Environment and Society, "*Biblical wilderness is defined as several different types of intense experiences such as the of stark need for food and water, isolation or a renewal, of encounters with God.*"

Do you see a parallel between the spiritual and natural wilderness? They both are places of desolation, drought, and little to no growth. I would describe living in a wilderness experience as a period when we lack intimacy with God. You're not spending quality time with God, you're not reading your Bible, and you're not praying or seeking His face. In other words, you are not doing anything to nurture or maintain your personal relationship with God, and the two of you are drifting apart.

Now that you have a clearer understanding of what a wilderness looks like, could you imagine living in one? During times of intimacy with the Lord, we passionately pursue Him. We have an insatiable desire to read our Bible, to please Him, and we keep Him first in our lives. However, when we are drying up spiritually, we start to become consumed with other relationships. if not addressed, this can move you right out of position in the Kingdom of God.

When I look back on what I was experiencing a few years ago, I was definitely going through a wilderness experience. I wasn't as close to the Lord as I used to be, and I wasn't spending time with Him like I had in the past. I wasn't praying or reading my Bible consistently, and I was experiencing a loneliness that I had never experienced before. I had allowed other things to take His place in my life. It was easier to pursue other relationships than to pursue God. If you were to take my spiritual temperature, I would have registered as lukewarm. Instead of being hot and on fire for the Lord, I had become lukewarm and complacent. Instead of coming home and getting into the Word of God, I would watch TV until it was time to go to bed. I no longer had a designated time to spend with the Lord. I gave more attention to my job than I did to the Lord. The only time I opened my Bible was for Sunday morning service and my weekly bible study group. I was a prime candidate for the wilderness.

One day, I stumbled upon an article by Pastor Jay Robison, and his words summarized exactly how I was feeling. *"The wilderness is full of loneliness, self-doubt, questioning, and despair. We feel knocked down and terribly alone."* While Pastor Robison described accurately what I was going through, I didn't know what I could do about it. How could I muster up enough strength to pull myself out of this lonely, self-doubting, dry place?

Medically speaking, the human body cannot function properly without enough water. Most doctors recommend that you drink at least half your body weight in water to remain properly hydrated. However, if you are in a place that is desolate and dry, and there is very little water, after three to five days, the body begins to become dehydrated, which will eventually lead to organ failure and other lethal consequences including death. The human body can go much longer without food, but eventually, that can also have lethal consequences.

As in the natural, so in the spirit. According to John 4:14, *"... whoever drinks the water I give them will never thirst. ... Indeed, the water I give them will become in them a spring of water welling up to eternal life."*. The scriptures refer to the <u>Word of God</u> as both our food and our water, and we need it daily to grow into spiritual maturity.

I was thirsty for God, but I wasn't asking Him for a drink of water. I wasn't going to the source Who could have easily quenched that thirst; instead, I just remained thirsty. Part of me yearned for God, wanted more of God. I wanted to spend more time with Him. I wanted to memorize more scripture so I could be better equipped to pray and tear down strongholds. I wanted to be used by God and make an impact for the Kingdom of God. But instead, I was in the driest season of my life. I was saved, and I loved the Lord and was living holy to the best of my ability. I talked to God and even sensed His Presence when I worshiped, but I didn't always sense that closeness we used to have. I was not as acquainted with the scriptures as I used to be. I didn't study anymore. I didn't pray like I used to. I felt complacent. Here I was, supposed to be the author of *Vertical Worship*, and yet I couldn't even get my own relationship with the Lord together!

I knew people would say, "You're being too hard on yourself; after all, God knows your heart," or, "Remember, we walk by faith, not by our feelings." Or one of my favorites, "You are one of the most spiritual people I know." And to that, I say thank you. The problem is this: I knew what my relationship with my Heavenly Father had been before I entered into the wilderness, and I knew what it looked like now. And once you have tasted the goodness of the Lord and ascended to a certain level with Him, you know what it feels like when you are no longer operating on that level.

I knew I was in trouble when I had gotten to where I couldn't quote scripture the way I used to. My prayers were repetitive; they were not coming from my heart, but from my head. I couldn't remember some of the more significate bible stories I used to know, and I no longer sensed the anointing on my life that I had experienced when I was on a higher level with God.

But how did I get here? How did I slip into complacency so badly? How did I go from hungering and thirsting for God, His Word and His Presence, to being satisfied with a mediocre life? The short answer is, I don't know. If I dig deeper, I can see where a few life experiences helped to propel me into the wilderness. I struggled to keep depression at bay so it would not overcome me, and I lived under tremendous stress on the job. A few years ago, I went through a life-changing move from one state to another, leaving friends, church, and relationships I treasured. And lastly, I entered into the world of care giving for my elderly parent, which required a great deal of my time. Ultimately, I got so busy with life that I began to take God for granted. I longed for those times when I had a hunger and thirst for the things of God. I wanted to cry out, *"I thirst with the deepest longings to love You more, with cravings in my heart that can't be described. (Psalm 63:1),"* but I was stuck in a rut. My wheels were spinning, but I wasn't going anywhere. And when I did pray to the Lord, I often felt that my words were falling on deaf ears. But the truth was that I wasn't ready to do the hard work of rebuilding my relationship with God.

If you sense that you are going through a dry season in your life, one of the first things you have to do is recognize what season you are in. Ecclesiastics 3:1 says, "To everything there is a season, and a time to every purpose under heaven." You would be amazed how many Believers don't even realize they are in a season of complacency. They are so used to coming and going that they have learned to operate on auto pilot. But if you know you are in a dry season and feel like you are going through a wilderness experience, then you can take some steps to get out of it. This is similar to the first steps in Alcoholics Anonymous—in order to be delivered from alcoholism, you must first admit you cannot control your addition and that you are an alcoholic. This requires that you be brutally honest with yourself no matter how much it hurts.

Take a few moments now and take your spiritual temperature and see if you are experiencing any of the following symptoms:

1) Lacking passion, affection, or devotion for God
2) Prayer is slacking or non-existent
3) Prayer life has become five-minute prayers spoken on the way to work
4) Putting more effort in maintaining relationships with others than your relationship with the Lord
5) Instead of having preeminence in your life, the Lord has taken second place
6) Spending more time on social media and/or watching TV than with the Lord
7) Spending more time working on your career than spending time with the Lord

Now I'm not saying that you cannot maintain other relationships, get on social media, watch TV, or aggressively pursue your career, but make sure that your EGO does not get in the way. EGO is an acronym meaning **E**asing **G**od **O**ut. Because if anything in your life begins to ease God out, it will be detrimental to your spiritual growth. Easing God out of your life will cause you to depend more on yourself and others than on God. It will affect your prayer life and your level of discernment will decrease. The Bible says in Matthew 4:4, *"It is written: 'Man shall not live on bread alone, but on every word that comes from the mouth of God.'"* In other words, we cannot be sustained by just natural food and water—no, it's the Word of God that is our true sustainer.

As Believers in Jesus Christ, we all go through dry seasons. Some of us go through them and come out on the other side stronger and go on to do exploits for God, while others never seem to make it out of their dry season and remain in limbo most of their Christian lives.

Are you sweating because you are working hard for the Kingdom by pursuing the Lord, or are you thirsty for more of God because you're in a dry season?

Did I Backslide?

*"Take care, brethren, that there not be in any one of you an evil, unbelieving heart that **falls away** from the living God."*
Hebrew 3:12 [NASB]

Definition: **back·slide** - to lapse morally or in the practice of religion; to revert to a worse condition

Back in 2016, I made a life-changing move from Texas to South Carolina. After a courageous battle with cancer, we lost my mother in 2012. I had the distinct honor to be with her as she took her last breath and transitioned to her glorious home in heaven. After her passing, I began traveling back and forth from Texas to South Carolina to visit my father. But as he was getting older and missing my mother, the Lord laid on my heart to relocate permanently to South Carolina to be closer to him. The transition was a smooth one. I got a job within two weeks, all my belongings arrived in one piece, and after searching for several months, I finally found a new church home.

While I did attempt to plug into my new church, I was not nearly as invested in ministry as I was back in Texas. There I was actively involved in dance ministry, finance ministry, hospital and hospice ministry, to name a few. Here in South Carolina, I joined the intercessory team, prison ministry and pursued my passion of visiting the sick and dance ministry, but this was so rare and not nearly as often as back in Texas. After a while, I felt myself going through the motions of a daily routine. I was "enduring" life and not "enjoying" it. I was paying more attention to the things of the world, like my job, watching my favorite reality shows, and surfing on the internet than I was to my relationship with the Lord, and this brought on tremendous guilt. I didn't leave God, but I wasn't pursuing Him either. I didn't like feeling this way. I felt half complete because I wasn't giving Him my all. I was not experiencing His peace or feeling His convictions like I used to. I wasn't going around the house praising God for the little things anymore. It was as if my light had gone out; I was merely existing, and my life was no longer a Christ-centered one.

I had entered into a wilderness experience, and I felt trapped.

Larnelle Harris wrote a song back in 1986 entitled "I Miss My Time With You," and these lyrics were becoming more and more of a reality to me.

I Miss My Time With You

There He was just waiting,
In our old familiar place
An empty spot beside Him,
Where once I used to wait
To be filled with strength and wisdom
For the battles of the day
I would have passed Him by again
If I didn't hear Him say

I miss my time with you
Those moments together
I need to be with you each day
And it hurts Me when you say
You're too busy,
Busy trying to serve Me
But how can you serve Me
When your spirit's empty
There's a longing in My heart
Wanting more than just a part of you
It's true, I miss My time with you
Songwriters: Larnelle Harris / Phill Mchugh

I first heard this song more than 30 years ago while still living in New York, and for a while, it became my song of conviction. Can you imagine the Lord God Almighty, El Shaddai, sharing His heart and telling you, *"I miss My time with you, and it hurts Me when you say that you are too busy trying to serve Me, but how can you serve Me, when your spirit is empty?"* Man, how this would bring such conviction to me, just to think that my busyness was hurting the heart of God. Not only my busyness was keeping me away from God, but my complacency was affecting my relationship with Him as well. Both of them were rather self-centered—it was all about me and my prosperity, my feelings, without giving any consideration to how the Lord was feeling.

This is why I appreciate the Holy Spirit so much. Even in the midst of my complacency, the Holy Spirit gently guided me back to reality, and my starving spirit once again began to hunger and thirst for more of God and less of myself. But if I allowed the complacency to linger too long, I would find myself right back in a dry season where I would lack the desire to pursue Him. It was during these times that I had to ask myself, "Did you backslide?" That was the last thing I wanted to do, but it was beginning to look like it.

To get some clarity, I looked up the definition of "backslide" and compared it to what I was experiencing.

*"The word **backslide**, in a Christian context, implies <u>movement away from Christ</u> rather than toward Him. A backslider is someone who is going the wrong way, spiritually. He is <u>regressing rather than progressing</u>. The backslider had at one time demonstrated a commitment to Christ or maintained a certain standard of behavior, but he has since <u>reverted to old ways</u>. Backsliding may manifest itself in several ways, e.g., dropping out of church, losing fervor for the Lord, walking away from a ministry or a family, or falling back into old habits."*

Going through a dry season can look like you have backslid, but the main difference between the two is that the backslider is moving away from God and reverting back to their old ways, whereas during a dry season, you maintain a relationship with God. It may not be as passionate as it once was, but you are still holding on to God. You still do the work of a Christian, but you do it almost robotically. What I was going through definitely had some backsliding qualities, but some of the major characteristics were not true for me. I did not revert to my old ways and walk away from the Lord, ministry, or the church. Instead, I was stuck in a rut, going through a spiritual battle for my life and not knowing which way to turn.

You can tell if you have backslid or are going through a dry season by asking yourself the following questions:

1) Has something shifted in your relationship with God?
2) Do you still talk to God?
3) Have you reverted back to your old ways before Christ (or picked up some new ones that do not glorify Christ)?
4) Are you still passionate about Christ and hunger for more of Him? If not, do you want to restore your relationship with God back to the passion you once experienced?
5) And most importantly, do you WANT TO get out of this wilderness experience or are you comfortable here?

These are hard questions where you have to be brutally honest with yourself. If you truly mean business, then you will be completely transparent with the Lord. I know it's hard, but it is so worth it. Not too long ago, I was you. I was wandering around in the wilderness searching for a way out, crying to God for a way out, and was looking for steps to make changes in my spiritual life, even if they were just baby steps.

Where are you right now in your life? Have you backslid and need to repent to the Lord and regain that relationship with Him? Or are you going through a wilderness experience and need to repent to the Lord for your laziness and ask that He rekindle that fire and passion for more of Him and less of yourself? Both experiences require repentance, which means to apologize to the Lord for your shortcomings and turn away from sin.

No matter where you are in life, God is there, waiting, willing, and desiring to hear from you because He loves you so much and wants to be in a healthy relationship with you again.

What Season Is It?

*"To everything there is a **season**, and a time to every purpose under the heaven"*
Ecclesiastes 3:1 [NIV]

Definition: **sea·son** - an indefinite period of time

The third chapter of Ecclesiastes gives us many examples of seasons we all face in life: times of birth, death, healing, weeping, and joy to name a few. What I love about God is that no matter what season we may find ourselves in, He is always there. He is an Omnipresent God, meaning that He is everywhere at the same time; therefore, we do not have to be fearful that we are going through these seasons alone.

Another thing I love about God is that He knew we would have "a time to break down and a time to build up." And in His infinite wisdom, He made provision for whatever season we may find ourselves in.

In the article "3 Reasons Why We Go Through Spiritually Dry Seasons" by JB Cachila, the author lists 3 main reasons why we as Christians go through dry seasons:

1) We disobey God.
2) We don't receive enough nourishment from God's Word and prayer.

3) We are transitioning from one season to another.

I believe that my dry season was a direct result of a combination of items number two and three. You know what, if I am going to be completely transparent, let's just throw in number one as well. I was disobedient because I did not stay in the Word of God, knowing that *"Man shall not live by bread alone, but by every **word** that proceeds out of the mouth of God."* I didn't respond to all those urgings the Lord was giving me. Because of my busyness, I was not getting enough nourishment from God's Word or spending the necessary time alone with Him to refuel, and because of my complacency, I was praying just enough to get by. And to top it all off, I was about to transition into another season of life—the fabulous sixties!

I was thirsty for God, but I wasn't asking for a drink of water from the Word of God. I wasn't going to the source, which could have easily quenched that thirst. I have gone through several dry seasons in my forty years walking with the Lord, but I was about to enter into a wilderness experience for the next five years that I had never experienced before. Through it all, I have never completely let go of the Lord's unchanging Hand, but I cannot confidently say that I was growing by leaps and bounds either.

So, what did I do? How did I get back to my intimate relationship with the Lord? How did I get my passion back? How did I create that hunger and thirst for Him and His Righteousness again?

I went back to the source. God.

After repenting for my lack of consistency and complacency, I asked Him to spark that same passion in me that I found when I was first saved.

How did I regain my intimate relationship with God after I had grown stale? I worshiped. How did I ignite that passion again when the ambers of my fire had grown faint? I worshiped. How did I maintain my sanity in the midst of a crazy mixed-up world? I worshiped.

As I shared in the introduction, in 2008 the Lord gave me a personal revelation on the topic of Vertical Worship. Now, over thirteen years later, as I found myself trying to navigate through my own wilderness experience, the Lord threw me a lifeline, but little did I realize that it would be my own book! I didn't know the Lord was going to use my book on Vertical Worship as a workbook to help me get out of this wilderness experience and back into a more peaceful, passionate relationship with my Savior, my Lord, and my best Friend.

First, in order to give you some context about why I feel the way I do and how I got here, let's go back to when I was first saved.

My Beginning

"...being confident of this very thing, that He *who has* **begun** a good work in you *will complete it until the day of Jesus Christ."*
Philippians 1:6 [NKJV]

Definition: **be·gin·ning** - the point at which something begins

Walking with the Lord is the most rewarding experience in my life. When I first came to the saving knowledge of Jesus Christ, I was twenty-one years old and in my last semester of college. I was living alone in Brooklyn, New York, after my parents relocated back to their hometown in the south. My testimony was not as bad as some. I cannot say that He delivered me from a wild life of partying, getting high, and sleeping around, because at the time, I didn't drink, smoke, or curse (and I still don't). I was just a young lady in college trying to get my degree and a good paying job upon graduation. I used to say I was a "good girl on my way to hell." Why? Because even though I faithfully attended church every Sunday, I had not accepted Jesus Christ as my personal Savior. After college, I continued living life, going to plays and dinner with friends and going out on dates. I had no real desire to get married, but I did like having a significant male in my life. I had a few a long-distance relationships, which I did not mind because I always felt marriage would come later. Eventually, after one too many broken relationships with men, I had reached a point where I did not enjoy my lifestyle any longer. I wanted a change, so I cried out, "Lord, help me!" One thing I knew from going to church all those years was that I could call on God in times of trouble. It was there, in the privacy of my small studio apartment, where the Lord swooped in and captured my attention.

He had already accepted me; now it was my turn to accept Him. I repented for my sins and accepted Him into my life as my personal Savior. The relationship was glorious! Almost instantaneously, I started reading the Bible, and it made sense. I started listening to Christian radio and was enjoying the teachings. I started going to a Pentecostal church, which was very different from my A.M.E. Methodist upbringing, and I was soaring!

As a preteen, our neighbor, Mrs. Samuels, would invite me to attend her Pentecostal church on Saturdays, and every time the Pastor would make an "altar call" for those who wanted to accept Jesus as their Personal Savior, I would be the first one at the altar. In my church, we had a "call to the altar" where we would be invited to the altar to pray for a few minutes and go back to our seats, so I would also go up to the altar to pray. At first, I did not feel any different at either church, because I did not sense the need to change. I had no problem with Jesus Christ, but I was confused. I didn't understand that I not only needed to say a prayer to God at the altar, but I had to invite Him into my life and turn away from my sin. The concept sounded easy after I was saved, but it didn't make sense before. But once I said "yes" to Jesus in my little apartment on Greene Avenue, He literally invaded my life in the best way.

Once planted in a church (I left the A.M.E. church and started going to a Pentecostal church), I started to drink the scriptures. I was so hungry and thirsty for God and God alone. I went to every service. I participated in every event. I learned how to fast, how to pray, and how to shut-in overnight with the Lord. It was at one of our shut-in services (where they literally lock the church doors at night and we pray all night long in shifts) where I was filled with the Holy Spirit and began speaking in tongues. This was the second-best thing that I had experienced besides salvation. I firmly believe it was the indwelling of the Holy Spirit that has kept me saved all these years. I'll share more about this experience in my chapter on the Holy Spirit.

The Great Epiphany (The Original One)

Do not conform to the pattern of this world, but be transformed by the renewing of your mind. Then you will be able to test and approve what God's will is—His good, pleasing and perfect will.
Romans 12:2 [NIV]

Definition: **epiph·a·ny** - an intuitive grasp of reality through something (such as an event) usually simple and striking

As I submerged myself in the things of God, I took extensive notes during service, and then I would type them out when I got home. Yes, I am a nerd! I reached a point of profound reverence, and even to this day, whenever I write about God in a pronoun format, I always capitalize the "You, Your, He, His and Him," even when I am quoting scriptures. I enrolled in Bible School. I studied, fasted, and prayed my way to graduation. I began to speak out about Christ and shared Him with my friends and family. I joined the usher board, hospital ministry, and the nursing home ministry, where I shared the gospel with the patients. But as I began to grow as a Christian, the Pentecostal experience was no longer enough for me. You see, besides getting into the Word and joining the church, I also had to give up a few things besides sin. Things like earrings and makeup and pants—all things that showed a more pious outer appearance, but had nothing to do with my heart.

Then I was introduced to my very first Integrity Hosanna cassette. Now, I know that I am dating myself, but I absolutely fell in love with worship music through cassette tapes. All this time, I had been singing hymns and traditional gospel music, which definitely had its place in my spiritual development, but when I was exposed to worship music, I almost did a 180. Once again, I found myself submerging into this new love. I started listening and singing any song I could get my hands on because the lyrics contained the Word of God. These songs not only drove me closer to God, but they also helped me with scripture memory.

Then I had my great epiphany (one of many). There are two basic camps of Christian music; **praise music** and **worship music** (we also have contemporary, jazz, hip-hop, etc., but at this season of my life, it was these basic two). Praise music was my "feel good music." **Praise music** rejoiced in the goodness of the Lord. It shared how the Lord brought us through, took us up the rough side of the mountain and made a way when there was no way out of our life situations. We sang it as story-telling or as Pentecostal foot stomping music, and after the choir finished, you were either up on your feet rejoicing, crying, or passed out on the floor from dancing! And I loved it.

But **worship music** was in a whole other realm. Worship music talked about God's attributes and who He was in my life. I was no longer talking about what He has done for me–which was a lot–but about how magnificent He was. How great He was. How much I loved Him. It was all about Him; I was taken out of the equation and

God was being magnified through the lyrics. Now we were singing about how awesome and great God was. We were incorporating scripture into the songs like "Great and Mighty is He," "Purify My Heart," "Let Us Exalt His Name," and "As the Deer Pants for the Water." I not only sang about it, but I began to believe that the Lord was my Shield, my Provider, and my Healer. I was that deer panting for water, wanting more of Him. I was hooked. Worship music literally changed my life, and I would never be the same again.

A Change in Religion

"If the **Son** *therefore shall make you* **free***, ye shall be* **free** *indeed"*
John 8:36 [KJV]

Definition: **change** - to make radically different; to make a shift from one to another

I was so happy with my newfound love in worship music and surprised to learn that this type of music had been out for years and sung all over the world while I was just getting the revelation. But then suddenly, church as I knew it wasn't the same. I began to hunger and thirst for more, and the church I was attending just could not quench my thirst. I was always told that you never outgrow your leadership. In other words, if you begin to grow and have fresh revelations about God and the Word of God, but your church is stuck in a rut, then it may be time for you to leave. Do not talk about the church; do not talk about the Man or Woman of God; instead, begin to seek God for clear direction and leave on good terms, and I did just that.

I began to internally question why I couldn't do certain things and yet still be a Christian. Questions like, why can't I wear pants? Why do I have to always wear a dress, even when riding a bike or attending a picnic? Why can't I wear jewelry? Where is the sin in that? And most importantly, why can't I get remarried?

Yes, I just laid another bombshell on you, didn't I? You see, while I was in my second year of college, I met and fell in love with a Nigerian student. After a whirlwind romance, he asked my father for my hand in marriage and proposed. We planned to get married at the end of school, but he graduated two years ahead of me and his student visa was expiring and he was considering going back home. So, with my bright idea, I suggested, "Why don't we elope secretly and then have the big event later?" We did the former, but never got around to doing the latter. We eloped a few days after his graduation, kept it a secret from my family, and resumed as an engaged couple. But by the end of the year, the bloom was off the rose and by the following year, we filed for an annulment.

Mind you, this all took place in my B.C. (before Christ) days, but once I was born again, my church doctrine taught that once married, always married. So even though I was legally annulled and single, for the first six years of my salvation, I never dated another man because I was told I had to believe God for my unsaved ex-husband's salvation and our reconciliation. Needless to say, this never happened, and this marriage thing was being held over my head like a bad dream.

A barrage of feelings ensued. I felt hurt, cheated, and trapped. How could a God of forgiveness forgive a murderer, but not forgive me for a stupid mistake made in my early twenties? I was stuck. I had never even had the experience of actually living with a man yet, nor had I experienced what a real marriage felt like (remember it was a secret, so I was still living with my parents at the time). But I was told that I had to believe God for "that man" and only him.

During this season, I watched some of my friends who also believed God for their ex-husbands' salvation and reconciliation, and they did get remarried. I went to a few of their weddings and wondered if mine would ever be manifested. Unfortunately, most of those reconciliations did not last, and secretly on the inside, I praised God for sparing me from such reconciliation.

All I can say is thank God for my personal relationship with Jesus. For it was God Himself through His Word who brought me out of bondage into His marvelous light. As I was beginning to sink in despair, He whispered in my ear, "*If the* **Son** *therefore shall make you* **free**, *ye shall be* **free** *indeed* (John 8:36)," and, "*There is therefore now* **no condemnation** *to them which are in Christ Jesus* (Romans 8:1)."

It was around this time when I was just discovering my newfound love for worship music that I also sensed in my spirit that it was time to leave my denomination. Finally, after months of praying and fasting and standing on God's Word, I mustered enough courage to leave the Pentecostal church and started attending a non-denominational church.

New Beginnings

*"Therefore, if any man be in Christ, he is a **new** creature: old things are passed away; behold, all things are become **new**."*
II Corinthians 5:17 [KJV]

Definition: **<u>new</u>** - having recently come into existence

Some people felt that the Pentecostal church was very restrictive, and it was. I couldn't wear pants, makeup, or earrings. I couldn't go to the movies or listen to secular music, but I will never criticize my Pentecostal experience. It was this experience that taught me how to pray, how to fast, how to step out on faith and believe God for miracles. It was there where I was filled with the Holy Spirit and went to Bible School, something I will never forget and will always be grateful for.

However, it finally came time for me to leave. I was ready to go deeper in the Lord, but I could no longer do it at my current church home.

Israel Houghton penned a song called "So Come" and the following words became my new model for spiritual growth: *"Oh God, that **ceiling** that we were trying to break through has now become the **floor** of a new dimension, another level, a deeper level, take us deeper."*

I loved my Pentecostal experience, but I had reached the ceiling of this experience and now it was time to enter into the floor of my new dimension.

After leaving the Pentecostal church, the Lord immediately led me to an awesome non-denominational church where my journey toward Vertical Worship truly began. The original name of the church was Household of Faith in Brooklyn, now known as Christian Cultural Center (CCC). At the time, it was a small, intimate church filled with the anointing which caused me to grow to another level in my relationship with God. When I started worshiping there, I was already in love with the Lord, but I started growing deeper and deeper in love with Him. One thing CCC knew how to do was to set the atmosphere for worship. It was there where I learned that the Holy Spirit loves an atmosphere of worship, and I experienced the Lord's love on a deeper level. Brokenness occurred during worship. Healing was manifested during worship. Deliverance and peace of mind were restored during worship. It was at this new dimension where I found another level of worship—dance.

The Sunday morning when I first saw Dance Ministry was life changing. I loved how the dancer moved with such grace and conviction, but it was the element of worship that took the dance to a whole other level. I was hooked. I was smitten. I was hungry for this new level of worship. Months later, when they posted the announcement for openings in the dance ministry, I leaped at the opportunity. There was an application process to be on the team, so

I took a form, and when I was finished, my application was filled with a bunch of nos.

- Do you have any dance experience? No
- Have you ever been a member of a dance team? No
- Are you currently taking dance classes? No

Mind you, I had never taken a dance class in my life. The only dance I knew was hip hop from the projects, but I felt compelled to join this team with no qualifications except a pure heart. Then finally there was a question on the application that I could answer in the affirmative:

- **What is your vision for Dance Ministry?**

At the time I didn't realize it, but my answer would become my lifelong motto for worship:

"My vision is simply this, to use dance as a mode of expression of my love and adoration for Jesus Christ."

And that sealed the deal; I was in. I was told to report to rehearsals the following week.

Dancing for the King

*"You turned my wailing into **dancing**; you removed my sackcloth and clothed me with joy."*
Psalm 30:11[NIV]

Definition: **dance** – to move one's body rhythmically, usually to music

Little did I know that this next chapter in my life would position me in ministry for the rest of my life. Whoever said dance ministry was easy—they lied. This ministry has been one of the most difficult yet rewarding ministries that I have ever had the privilege to serve in. I thank God that my initial exposure to dance ministry was one of excellence and spirituality and not just performative and showy. I learned so much by being a part of dance ministry at CLC, but my main takeaway was that it is a very powerful ministry that can shift the direction of any service if ministered under the anointing.

It was this newfound passion that led me to worship the Lord in a new and deeper way. For you see, I was not only worshiping God with my mouth or by the lifting of my hands. I was now worshiping God with my entire body. It was this realization that caused me to live a more consecrated life before my King. If He was going to use me to shift the atmosphere and lead people into a deeper realm of worship, then I had to be the first partaker and live a life worthy of such an honor.

Dancing for the Lord definitely had its challenges, both spiritual and natural. The natural challenges were basically training this sinful flesh to submit and move the way the choreography had intended—but because I joined dance ministry at the ripe old age of 29 (most ballerinas retire between 30-40 years old), my body was locked into position, and it was very hard to minister the way I really wanted to. But as hard as the natural limitations were, nothing could compare to the spiritual attacks that came along with this calling. There were times when I felt sick right after ministry. I would feel beaten up physically and it would take two days to recover. The temptations became greater and the physical and spiritual attacks were endless.

Any time you take a stand for righteousness, the enemy is not too far away. So, I had to take a stand and dig my roots deep. Not only did I excel in dance ministry as a member of the team, but when I relocated to Texas, the Lord saw fit to elevate me to the position of dance leader. Now I not only had the weight of responsibility of my own ministry but those whom the Lord entrusted me to serve in ministry as well. It was hard work, but I would not have traded it for the world. Soon, I was not only leading a dance ministry; I was also hosting national dance conferences, creative arts conferences, and creative arts leadership summits. It was during the preparation of one such conference when the Lord finally revealed to me the Vertical Worship concept.

Vertical Worship – The Principles

"But the hour is coming, and now is, when the true worshipers will worship the Father in spirit and truth; for the Father is seeking such to worship Him. God is Spirit, and those who worship Him must worship in spirit and truth."
John 4:23-24 [NKJV]

Definition: **prin·ci·ple** - a fundamental truth that serves as the foundation for a system of belief or behavior

The word **worship** means to give adoration, homage, loving devotion, respect, and reverence to a divine being. For all those who love God, the Lord should be the chief focal point of our worship. I believe that what the Lord is looking for are those who will worship Him with reckless abandonment, unashamedly, purely and without selfish motives. If you want to grow in God, worship must be a part of your fundamental existence.

As I shared at the beginning of the book, when the Lord revealed the concept of Vertical Worship to me, I was excited to share it with the world, but first, I had to explain what it meant. Vertical Worship has God as its primary focus. All of our praise, adoration, respect, devotion, and attention are aimed directly to Him. The more we worship Him, the more we are set free from the stronghold of this world.

In my pursuit to worshiping God vertically, He originally gave me eight (8) principles to follow. However, after going through my wilderness experience, the Lord added an additional four (4) principles that helped me to experience greater victory as He led me out of the wilderness completely. They are very basic principles, but if you implement them into your daily life, you will not only maintain your connection to the Lord, but you will also develop a deeper intimacy with Him. I will be discussing these principles in greater detail further in the book.

Is My worship Really Vertical?

"When my heart is overwhelmed, lead me to the rock that is higher than I"
Psalm 61:2 [NKJV]

Definition: **ver·ti·cal** - perpendicular to the plane of the horizon: upright

Vertical Worship displays the love affair between the creation and the Creator. Most people on today's reality TV shows say they are looking for love. The desire to be loved by another human being is in our DNA. It is not unusual to want to be loved, to get married and have children. But unfortunately, we, me included, have put this quest for love above the desire to be loved by God.

Why should we worship vertically? Because that was God's original intent. He designed us to worship. We are creatures of worship. But besides all that, we should worship vertically because He is worthy of our worship. I know it's cliché, but we are living in a wicked and perverse generation, and we need someone we can look to for peace, comfort, and just to tell us everything is going to be okay. We need to keep our eyes on Jesus; otherwise, we can easily go crazy. We need a focal point higher than ourselves.

This was one of the hardest things to do while I was going through my wilderness experience—staying focused—but the sweet

Holy Spirit always gently directed me to keep my mind on Jesus. When you are going through a dry season, you can be easily distracted because you are so depleted of liquids, you begin to lose your strength and tire easily. You lose your fight and stamina, and all you want to do is lay down and go to sleep. I would get up and go to work, but when I came home, I didn't feel like doing anything except watching the news, which was depressing in itself.

To be honest, what kept me going initially was my Thursday night bible study. During this season of my life, two of my dear friends Pam and Jimmy Rast hosted a weekly bible study in their home, and it was during this time when I was surrounded by other strong believers that I felt connected with the Lord. It caused me to stay focused on Him and it also reminded me how much He really loved me. I faithfully went to church and served on the hospitality team, yet the passion I had once experienced was waning. It was these bible studies held in a safe and intimate setting at the Rasts' home where the Lord nurtured me with the Word of God.

I did these things in order to stay connected to the Body of Christ, because even though I was going through a spiritual drought, I didn't want to become completely disconnected from God. I knew I needed to keep myself hydrated with the Word of God any way I could get it.

I had to practice what I had preached all these years. I had to keep my worship vertical.

Worshiping in The Wilderness - It's My Turn Now

*"O God of my life, I'm lovesick for you in this weary **wilderness.**"*
Psalm 63:1 [TPT]

Definition: **wil·der·ness** - an uncultivated place.

uncultivated - not developed by training or effort, growing or developing without care

As I stated in chapter one, as humans, we go through many seasons of life. Some seasons bring great joy while others bring immense pain. The key is to know what season you are in, and learn how to navigate through that season.

When it comes to your intimacy with God, there will be times of fluctuation. There may be times when you are on fire for God and other times when you may feel distant from Him. In my over forty years walking with God, I have learned to always remain transparent with Him. Always communicate with Him no matter how you are feeling. Never shut Him out. Always remain completely open and honest with Him. For example, if you feel lousy one day, tell Him. If you don't feel the passion you once had, let Him know. He is concerned about you. ALL OF YOU. One thing I learned about God early on is that He is **consistently consistent**. When He said that He would never leave us or forsake us, He meant it. God is not a man that He should lie (Numbers 23:19).

The worst thing you can do is cut off the line of communication with Him, because then you will create an opening for the enemy to start whispering in your ear that you are all alone and God doesn't care about you, when in actuality, God cares for your entire well-being (see Psalm 139, Matthew 10:30-32).

Joyce Myers wrote a powerful book years ago entitled *The Battlefield of the Mind.* In it she talks about how our biggest challenge is not necessarily the enemy of our souls. Most often, the battle comes from within, and it starts with our thought life. Romans 12:2 tells us "Do not be conformed to this world, but be transformed by the renewal of your mind, then you will be able to test and approve what God's will is—His good, pleasing and perfect will."

This is so crucial when going through a dry season in your life, because your mind is the first thing the enemy will attack. He will have you questioning every decision, every belief, every idea you have. He will flood your mind with unnecessary thoughts. You will find yourself thinking about everything but God. You will find that you are in the fight for your life. I know this to be true because I have experienced these mind games and I had to press through and persevere.

So, this is me, worshiping in the wilderness.

How I Worship Vertically in the Wilderness

*"Daily I will **worship** You passionately and with all my heart."*
Psalm 63:4 [TPT]

Definition: **wor·ship** - to honor or show reverence for a divine being

In my first book, I taught that Vertical Worship is not something you put on in the morning and take off at night. Worshiping God should be the lifestyle of every believer. But often times, Believers do not know what to do or where to start when it comes to worshiping the Lord. We often mistake praise for worship, depending on our denomination, and truth be told, we may not ever quite get to enjoy the awesome experience of worshiping God. Praising God is both a wonderful and very necessary part of our relationship with Him. It's letting Him know how much you appreciate Him for all He has done for you. This reminds me of the story of the ten lepers in Luke 17:11-19. Jesus healed all ten of them as they left to show themselves to the priest, but they were so excited about their healing that only one of them went back to say thank you. Even Jesus was shocked at the level of unappreciation.

Could you imagine being in a relationship with someone who is constantly helping you, blessing you, and providing for you and you never take the time to stop and thank them, never tell them how much you appreciate them? That would be a one-sided relationship and both offensive and discouraging to the one who is always providing the help. Therefore, it is very important to give God the praise He so richly deserves every single day.

Worship, however, is different from praise. It goes past thanking God for our many blessings and takes us in a deeper realm with Him. I always say that worship is talking to God about God. I am out of the equation. I am no longer thanking Him for what He has done for me personally; I am now telling Him how wonderful He is, how magnificent He is. It's all about Him and not about me.

Worshiping God does not require a congregation, an organ, or a psalmist. Although they help to set the atmosphere for worship, we must learn how to set our own atmosphere. You can worship God anytime and anyplace. Worship must come from a place of intimacy. Merriam-Webster describes intimacy as something of a personal or private nature; however, I love how Bishop T.D. Jakes put it in one of his teachings on the topic. He said that the word "intimacy" can be pronounced as *"into – me – see"*, or "see into me." I thought this was so profound that I have changed my mindset to this definition every time I think about intimacy with the Lord.

When I say I want to be intimate with the Lord, I'm saying that I want to go further and deeper in my relationship with Him. I want to go past the Sunday morning ritual of going to Sunday school and church service. I want to go past the hymnals, long pews, and electric organs. I want to be transparent enough for Him to see into me down to my core. I want to cut out all the pomp and circumstance and be totally open and honest with the Lord, allow Him to search my heart and cut away anything that displeases Him. Now that's true intimacy.

It was with this type of intimacy that I originally wrote the principles of Vertical Worship, because I strongly believed they would help those who were seeking to strengthen or deepen their intimacy with the Lord.

If you are going to teach on an experience, I am convinced that you need to have already gone through it or need to be currently going through it. This allows you to speak from a place of knowledge and authority.

As I was going through my own wilderness experience, I often felt like I was drifting away from God more than toward Him. During that time, I found these principles to be life-changing. Once I applied them to my life, they helped me stay afloat, so much so that the Lord taught me four additional principles to give me that extra push out of the wilderness and into a more abundant life.

For the next several chapters, I'll share these twelve (12) principles and the lessons I learned while I was going through the wilderness. I want to share both the rough times and the good times to encourage you that you, too, can walk out of your wilderness season and into victory.

Here are the principles I will share with you:
1. Knowing God
2. Dying to self
3. Practicing His Presence
4. Acknowledging His Deity
5. Acknowledge Personage of the Holy Spirit
6. Tell Him you love Him often
7. Sing love songs to Him
8. Develop a lasting Friendship with Him
9. Don't isolate yourself
10. Bathe yourself in the Word of God
11. Exercise—start moving
12. PRAY—Talk to God

Principle #1 - Knowing God

*"That I may **know** Him and the power of His resurrection, and the fellowship of His sufferings, being conformed to His death."*
Philippians 3:10 [NKJV]

Definition: **know** - to have understanding of **Knowing** - having or reflecting knowledge, information, or intelligence

Whenever we enter a relationship with another person, whether it be doctor/patient, employer/employee, teacher/student, or a romantic one, they all require one initial component—getting to know each other. One of the main differences in our human relationships versus our divine relationship with God is that in the human relationship, we are both trying to get to know each other. However, in our divine relationship with God, He already knows all there is to know about us down to the minute detail (see Psalm 139). In this relationship, we need to take the time and get to know who God really is—His character, what He likes and dislikes and how to better serve Him.

Knowing God is one of the most natural yearnings of the human soul. For centuries, man has been seeking for a "higher power" to worship. Whether it be a manmade statue or a mysterious being, man longs to have a "god" in their lives. However, the devil understands what a yielded heart to the Lord will do to his kingdom; therefore, he will try to enter a person's life as early as possible and attempt to hinder man's natural desire to know and commune with God. Sin separates man from God, and ever since the garden, mankind has been trying to get back into the right relationship with God. God is not hiding from us. He isn't so high that He is unobtainable. But the enemy of our souls wants you to believe that God isn't nearby. He wants you to believe that God is too busy saving the world to deal with your issues. But how many of you know that the devil is a liar, and the truth is not in him (John 8:44)? For the bible says that the Lord is near to the brokenhearted and that He is near to all who call upon Him (Psalm 34:18, Psalm 145:18).

I love Philippians 3:10. It was my go-to scripture in my early years with Christ and it still rings true today. But after taking a closer look at Philippians chapter 3, I realized how much of a commitment Paul was trying to convey to us, the Church. He was warning us to put no confidence in the flesh, to only place our confidence in Christ (v3). Look at the scripture verses that precede verse 10: *"⁷ But whatever were gains to me I now consider loss for the sake of Christ. ⁸ What is more, I consider everything a loss because of the surpassing worth of **knowing Christ Jesus my Lord**, for whose sake I have lost all things. I consider them garbage, that I may gain Christ ⁹ and be found in Him, not having a righteousness of my own that comes from the law, but that which is through faith in Christ— the righteousness that comes from God on the basis of faith."*

In other words, all the knowledge that I have acquired throughout my lifetime is worth nothing compared to what I can gain through knowing Christ. For His sake, I consider everything else garbage, that I may gain Christ and be found in Him. This became such a powerful revelation to me. I do not believe the scripture is teaching against gaining knowledge as we know it, because we all need to go to school and gain as much knowledge as we can in order to be successful in life. I think the Lord is trying to convey that we can gain all the knowledge in the world, but if we don't couple that with God, if it doesn't help me deepen my relationship with Him, then it's garbage to me. It's worthless. Christ must be the first object in my quest for knowledge, and everything else is second.

So, when I quote the scripture, *"That I may know Him... and the power of His resurrection, and the fellowship of His sufferings, being conformed to His death,"* it now takes on a greater and a deeper meaning to me. It is no longer a cute little bible verse that can easily be memorized and be rattled off without understanding the magnitude of what I am saying. Yes, I want to know Him. **Every facet and every nuance** of Him. But of course, that would take a lifetime of walking with the Lord, sitting at His feet, and talking to Him. But I also must realize that out of all the knowledge that I have gained in my lifetime, nothing surpasses the worth of knowing Christ Jesus. This thought gives me a deeper reverence toward Him.

Throughout my dry seasons, the desire to know God never waned. I never got tired of listening to teachings about Jesus. I never got tired of sitting silently in His Presence. As a matter of fact, I preferred it. There is nothing like waking up in the morning before the neighborhood starts stirring and sitting in your meeting place with the Lord. It brings peace and clarity.

But while I was going through my wilderness experience, even though I wanted to know more about Him, I wasn't actively pursuing Him. I was merely existing. I was doing just enough to stay afloat. I wasn't passionately pursuing Him like the deer pants for the water. I was lukewarm, and we all know how the Lord feels about lukewarmness.

I knew that the only way to really know God was through the Word of God, yet the wilderness had such a grip on me that the thing I knew to do, I did not. I remembered when I was first saved and how I pursued God so relentlessly. He rewarded me by revealing the different sides of His character as I grew in His grace. I longed for those times again; I wanted more of God and less of myself. I was miserable and there was only one way out: I had to shake off this compliancy and get back into the Word of God. It is His Word that brings us clarity. It is His Word that reveals God's heart. It's His Word that helps us understand who God really is.

If I was going to take my relationship with God seriously, then I needed to take my commitment, my confessions, and my desire to know Him seriously.

I realized that I must pursue Him through His Word in order to get out of this wilderness. I had to get the Word of God deep down inside me by any means necessary. If I could not read the Word, I would listen to it.

It was then I realized that I had a very short attention span! I was right smack in the middle of the wilderness, the Lord was handing me a lifeline to get myself out of the wilderness, yet I was barely holding on to it.

So I went back to the basics. First, I had to admit that I was in the wilderness and needed help. Next, I had to realize that only God's Word could lead me out. It was then that He led me to this plan of attack:

1) Change my bible translation to something that would resonate with me more.
2) Start a scripture memory program (my memory was not what it used to be).
3) Download the audible version of the Bible so I could listen to it while driving, working, and while drifting off to sleep.

Implementing these three things into my daily routine was crucial to beginning my journey out of the wilderness.

This scripture must now be my reason for living: "*I consider everything a loss because of* **the surpassing worth of knowing Christ Jesus my Lord**, *for whose sake I have lost all things.* **I consider them garbage**, *that I may gain Christ* [9] *and be found in Him.*"

Knowing God is a lifetime achievement. It does not come overnight, and neither should it. The best part of knowing God is the journey to knowing Him.

Principle #2 - Die to Self

"I have been crucified with Christ. It is no longer I who live, but Christ who lives in me. And the life I now live in the flesh I live by faith in the Son of God who loved me." Galatians 2:20 [NKJV]

Definition: **self** - a person's essential being that distinguishes them from others

Colossians 3:3 says that if you name the name of Christ, "you are dead and your life is hid with Christ in God," but during my wilderness experience, I realized very quickly that it's hard to keep that dead man in the grave. I was no longer a "dead man walking" as I described in my earlier book, but I was still walking in my flesh and very much alive.

Dying to self is a very conscientious thing. When we talk of "dying to self" as a Christian, this means dying to your old sinful nature. Dying to the big three: lust of the flesh, lust of the eye and the pride of life. II Corinthians 5:17 says it best: *"Therefore if any man be in Christ, he is s new creature: old things are passed away, behold, all things are become new."*

By accepting Christ into your life, you are saying, "I do not want to live a <u>self-centered</u> life; instead, I want to live a <u>Christ-centered</u> life." You have to be willing to lay yourself on the altar of sacrifice and allow the Lord to cut away those things in your heart that would cause you to go back to a life of sin. I once heard a preacher say,

"The problem with a living sacrifice is that they keep getting off the altar," and that's so true. We often equate the altar as a place of sacrifice, a place of pain, and we might not be ready to give up that much control of our lives just yet.

In the book *Hinds Feet in High Places* by Hannah Hurnard, the main character, Much Afraid, comes to a point where she is about to transition to her new identity as Grace and Glory. But before she can walk in that new transformation, there is one pivotal hurtle she must overcome—laying down her life on the altar. She admits that she doesn't have the strength to tie herself to the altar, so she asks the Good Shepard, who is representative of the Lord, to bind her to the altar. "Will You bind me to the altar in some way so that I cannot move? I would not like to be found struggling while the will of my Lord is done."

Oh Lord, how this story still gets to me so many years later! Like Much Afraid, I had to literally ask the Lord to tie me to the altar. I had to give Him complete and full permission to remove anything from my heart that was hindering me from becoming 100% devoted to Him. This wasn't another religious cliché. These weren't empty words recited on a Sunday morning during the call to altar. This was real and heartfelt. It was necessary for my survival.

While I was in the wilderness, I often wondered if I was dead or alive to the things of God. I couldn't figure out my value in the Kingdom anymore. I felt empty inside, but to be honest, I was still very full of self. I wasn't making room for more of Him and less of myself. Instead, I was allowing the flesh to do whatever it wanted (within reason, of course).

In order to truly live for the Lord, I had to first die for the Lord. I had to come to the end of myself for Christ to truly rule and reign in my life. I had to pick up my cross and follow Him. I had to become that dead man walking—dead to self and alive to the things of Christ. According to Colossians 3:3, "*I had to set my affections on things above because I am dead and my life is hidden with Christ.*"

Dying to self is a difficult thing to do, but it was also very necessary if I was to grow in Christ and get out of the wilderness. It took and is still taking much prayer, many tears, and a repentant heart. I admit that I have not reached 100% yet, but I am well on my way.

So how does one die to self? How do you get to the point where **"I'm crucified with Christ yet I no longer live, but Christ who lives in me?"** If we follow the example of Much Afraid in Hinds Feet in High Places, it sounds like this will require major surgery!

1. **The first thing you can do to curb the appetite of the flesh is to starve it.** Or, as we say in the Christian world, **fast.** Fasting is the number one way to keep the flesh under subjection. WARNING—fasting is a tool not only used by Christians; it is also used by the medical profession as well as non-Christian organizations. Therefore, when you are denying the flesh by fasting, make sure that you are supplementing yourself with the Word of God. You must fast

with purpose. In this instance, you are going before God and asking Him for a closer walk with Him. Some may have to ask Him to help them get deliverance from an addiction. Or you may have to ask Him to reveal what is hindering you from getting out of the wilderness. Idealistically, when you are sitting down to a meal, you should use that as a time to pray. **Remember,** if you do not include prayer and the Word in your fasting, all you are doing is getting skinny. God must be your focal point.

2. **Curb your appetite for worldly pleasures.** No, I'm not coming for your favorite television shows or worldly music—or am I? I Corinthians 10:23 says, *"All things are lawful for me, but all things are not expedient: all things are lawful for me, but all things edify not."* Meaning, "Everything is permissible, but not everything is beneficial" (Berean Study Bible). In other words, just because you don't see in the Bible not to do a thing, doesn't mean that you should partake in it. This world has a lot of "shiny objects" to offer that are very, very appealing to our flesh, but the barometer should be, "does it glorify God, or does it bring me any closer to Him?" Or here's another one: "Does participating in it or looking at it constantly draw my attention away from God?" These are hard questions that you must ask yourself, and you must be totally honest with

yourself and with God if you truly want to be set free and not dominated by your flesh.

3. **Put yourself under subjection of the Holy Spirit.** This one is done more by faith and not by sight. Since you cannot physically see the Holy Spirit, how can you put yourself under His subjection? The short answer is to just ask Him to take control of your life. Invite Him in. Surrender your desires to Him. This is something you can do during worship or during your personal prayer time. One thing I learned early in my Christian walk with the Lord is to be brutally honest with Him and He in turn will be brutally honest with me. Surrender to Him and He will guide and direct you out of so many unnecessary situations. Talk to Him and He will talk to you. It's that simple, but it does require a degree of faith to know that He is there, listening to you, caring for you, and concerned about you. *"...for he that cometh to God must believe that He is, and that He is a rewarder of them that diligently seek Him"* (Hebrews 11:6).

I once read in an article called "What Does it Mean to Set Your Mind on Things Above?" by Candice Lucey. She said, "Dying to self is like deleting the hard drive of your former self and rebooting fresh with a blank slate. You need to imitate Christ in order to relearn how to live." You can see this confirmed in Ephesians 4:22-24, *"You were taught, with regard to your former way of life,* **to put off your old self***, which is being corrupted by its deceitful desires;* [23] *to be* *made new in the attitude of your minds;* [24] *and* **to put on the new self**, *created to be like God in true righteousness and holiness." (NIV)*

What both the author and the scriptures are telling us is that we must get rid of our old lifestyle, our old mindsets, and our old way of doing things in order to be receptive to the new lifestyle we will find in Christ Jesus.

But like anything else that is valuable to you, it will take work. It will take discipline and a "want to" attitude, but it can be done. More importantly, if you want to get out of the wilderness that you may be facing right now, you must go through this process.

Read the lyrics to the song below by Pete McAllen and see if you can identify with it. If so, take some time and get before the Lord and pray these words to Him, letting Him know that you give Him your life, you refuse Him nothing, and you chose to die to yourself and live for Him.

Die to Myself - by Pete McAllen

I give my life to do Your will
Without delay, unreservedly
Refuse You nothing, I give myself
Seek You with all, and everything I am
Humbly I come before Your throne
Knowing You are Almighty King
Humbly I come before Your throne
Knowing Your mercy draws me in
I die to myself and I live for You
Whatever You ask Lord, I am Yours
Lay down my life to follow You
Whatever You ask Lord, I am Yours

I die to myself and I live for You
Whatever You ask Lord, I am Yours
Lay down all else to follow You
Whatever You ask Lord, I am Yours

by Pete McAllen on I Hear Your Voice (2014)

Principle #3 - Practice His Presence

*"I overflow with praise when I come before You, for the anointing of Your **presence** satisfies me like nothing else.* Psalm 63:5 [TPT]

Definition: **pres·ence** - the state or fact of existing, occurring, or being present in a place or thing

Practicing God's Presence is being cognizant of His Presence throughout the day. This awareness of His Presence has got to be the number one thing that helped me during my wilderness experience. Some of you may find this comical, but it's true; I am so aware of God's presence that every time I belch, even when I'm alone, I always say "Excuse me, Father." I am so conscious of His omnipresence that no matter where I am or who I am with, I know that God is there also. We are not just in God's presence at church or after a highly anointed worship service. No, God is everywhere at the same time. He is in every situation, every room, every car, and every house. He's behind every door, in every bathroom stall, and at every secret rendezvous. The Psalmist asked the question, *"Where can I flee from your presence?"* (Psalm 139:7b NIV) and the answer is NOWHERE.

Joshua 1:1 says, *"Be strong and of good courage; do not be afraid, nor be dismayed, **for the Lord your God is with you wherever you go.**"* Therefore, no matter how disconnected you feel, God is right there. He is honoring His part of the deal; now we must honor ours and always stay connected to Him. Remember, we walk by faith, not by our feelings.

One scripture I have held on to throughout my Christian walk, which can be both comforting and a bit alarming, is Psalm 139. Let's take a closer look at verses 1-8:

O LORD, You have searched me and known *me*.

² You know my sitting down and my rising up;

You understand my thought afar off.

³ You comprehend my path and my lying down,

And are acquainted with all my ways.

⁴ **For *there is* not a word on my tongue**,

But behold, **O LORD, You know it altogether**.

⁵ You have hedged me behind and before,

And laid Your hand upon me.

⁶ *Such* knowledge *is* too wonderful for me;

It is high, I cannot *attain* it.

⁷ **Where can I go from Your Spirit?**

Or where can I flee from Your presence?

⁸ **If I ascend into heaven, You *are* there**;

If I make my bed in hell, behold, You *are there*.

Verse 2 tells me that God is eavesdropping on my thoughts. Talk about a lack of privacy! But seriously, the scripture continues to talk about how God is acquainted with all our ways. God knows us through and through, and there is nowhere we are that He is not there also. I think the faster we come to this realization and come into agreement with the idea that God knows and understands us down to the minute detail, the more we will *"straighten up and fly right"* as my grandmother used to say.

Unfortunately, I think we as Believers often take God's Presence for granted, because if we truly believe that He is everywhere and can hear everything we say, see, and do, then we would be living our lives much differently—that is, if we really wanted to please Him. Even though I sometimes felt alone, in despair, or even forgotten, never once did I not sense the Presence of God near me, nor did I stop thirsting for His Presence.

There were times in the wilderness that I felt alone, in despair, and even forgotten. I knew the Lord hadn't left me, but I didn't feel His closeness. And that caused me to panic. I had always enjoyed being in the presence of the Lord, but suddenly I was thrust into a world of life without His tender touch. To go from having sweet communion with the Lord to not sensing His presence was unbearable. Living life outside of God's Presence felt like I was living without my best friend.

If I could suggest one thing to those who are going through a spiritually dry season right now, it would be to stay in His Presence. Never let Him go! Life is hard when you are right smack in the middle of God's will; can you imagine life outside of His will? I cherish the Presence of God. I protect the Presence of God, and I can't image life without His Presence in it.

The following are some tips that helped me during those times when I was battling with my flesh to maintain my intimacy with God:

1) I reminded myself Who God really is in my life and how He has never failed me all these years.
2) I thought about Him often, realizing that I cannot do anything without His divine intervention.
3) I constantly reminded myself of His omnipresence. He was always with me. I had to remind myself of His promise never to leave me, never to forsake me.

a) I listened to scripture-oriented music to help me stay focused on the Lord.
b) I sang worship songs to let Him know how much He meant to me.
c) I played worship music or listened to a teaching message on CD in my car on my way to and from work. These days, this is so easy to do, because you can find anointed songs, teachings, or scriptures on You Tube and play them through your phone.
d) I relied on the Holy Spirit daily.
e) I praised God for His goodness and for still meeting my needs—especially during a pandemic!
f) I continued to intercede for others (which means I had to talk to God).

g) I de-cluttered my mind and pressed into His Presence. To be honest with you, this one is the most difficult to do. Whenever I want to spend some quality time with the Lord, my mind races a hundred miles an hour, and I had to rid my mind of distractions before I could even begin. In this instance, praying out loud or singing God a love song helps me to divert my attention back to the Lord.

These are just some of the things you can do to help pull yourself out of a dry season of your life.

The bottom line is, I had to fall in love with the Lord all over again. I had to be completely honest with Him about where I was and where I wanted to be. When I didn't know the words to say, I would echo the words from an anointed worship session I just heard and make declarations to the Lord like, "I want to be overwhelmed by Your Presence, Lord," and, "You haven't failed me yet, and You never will. You are incapable of it. Thank You for Your indestructible and immutable Presence."

We should get excited about our meeting times with the Lord and wait with expectation. Even though He is always there, I still set a specific time and place to intentionally meet with Him, and I love it! Just to be in His presence again, wanting to spend time with Him—it's like when you are in love and you think about that special person all the time and plan a secret rendezvous to meet with them again. That's the way I feel about the Lord. He is the lover of my soul, and

I love Him with all my heart and soul. We're a match made in heaven.

The many benefits of God's Presence include peace, joy, patience, and times of refreshing. I ran across this quote from Benny Hinn that rings true about God's Presence to me, and I hope it does for you as well:

"The practice of the presence of the Lord begins when Jesus becomes more real to us than our problems, our families, our troubles, and even more real than life itself. At that moment, it is all about Jesus."— Benny Hinn, <u>Mysteries of the Anointing</u>

Principle #4 - Acknowledge the Personage of the Holy Spirit

"Do you not know that your bodies are temples of the Holy Spirit, who is in you, whom you have received from God? You are not your own; you were bought at a price. Therefore, honor God with your bodies." 1 Corinthians 6:19-20 [NIV]

Definition: **ac·knowl·edge** - to recognize the rights, authority, or status of

The Holy Spirit has often been the most neglected person of the Holy Trinity. We praise God, sing love songs to Jesus, and at times the Holy Spirit receives an honorable mention. Benny Hinn in his book *Good Morning Holy Spirit* hit the nail on the head. He quoted an experience he had when he attended one of Kathleen Kuhlman's services:

She was sobbing...and said with such agony, "Please...don't grieve the Holy Spirit." Then she said, "Don't you understand? He's all I've got. Don't wound the one I love."

In my church, the pastor talked about the Holy Spirit, but not like this. His references had to do with the gifts of tongues or prophesy, not that He's my closest, most personal, most intimate, most beloved friend. Kathryn Kuhlman was telling me about a person that was more real than you or I.

Is that powerful or what? When you get a chance, I encourage you to get Benny Hinn's book *Good Morning Holy Spirit* and also look up Kathryn Kuhlman's teachings on the Holy Spirit.

As I grow in my walk with the Lord, I have greatly depended on the Holy Spirit. Like Benny Hinn mentioned above, He's not just a reference to speaking in tongues or prophesy—no, He's more than that. He's the third member of the Holy Trinity. Not a day goes by when I don't receive clear direction from the Holy Spirit regarding some of the simplest tasks, such as which way I should drive to work in the morning or not to forget my bank card as I am walking out the door. Sometimes He will direct me to visit someone when they are at their lowest. And to be completely transparent, it was the Holy Spirit who directed me to write this book.

In order to understand the Holy Spirit and how important He is to our lives as Christians, let's go back to when He was first introduced to us in the scriptures.

Old Testament's promise of the Holy Spirit

"And there shall come forth a rod out of the stem of Jesse, and a Branch shall grow out of his roots: And the spirit of the LORD shall rest upon him, the spirit of wisdom and understanding, the spirit of counsel and might, the spirit of knowledge and of the fear of the LORD;" Isaiah 11: 1-2

Jesus promises to send us the Holy Spirit

*"If you love Me, keep My commandments. And I will pray the Father, and He will give you another Helper, that He may abide with you forever— the **Spirit of truth,** whom the world cannot receive, because it neither sees Him nor knows Him; but you know Him, for He dwells with you and will be in you."* John 14:15-17

The manifestation of the Holy Spirit [The Holy Spirit came on the day of Pentecost fifty days after the resurrection and ten days after the ascension of Jesus Christ]

*"But you shall receive power when **the Holy Spirit** has come upon you; and you shall be witnesses to Me in Jerusalem, and in all Judea and Samaria, and to the end of the earth."* Acts 1:8

After three years of intense ministry, Jesus announced that it was time to go back to His Father in heaven. You can imagine the despair His followers were experiencing, but being the gracious God that He is, Jesus let them know that He would not leave them comfortless. He was going pray to the Father to not only send Help, but One who would stay with them forever. Now who can give a better job reference that Jesus Christ?

Jesus went on to be crucified and buried, but as declared in scripture, He ROSE on the 3rd day—hence why we celebrate Easter. He walked the earth for another forty days and then ascended into Heaven (Thess 4:14), but ten days later, the blessed Holy Spirit was introduced into the earth realm, where He is still residing today to do the work that Jesus promised, to empower us to continue to do the work of witnessing and setting captives free.

*"When the Day of Pentecost had fully come, they were all with one accord in one place. ² And suddenly there came a sound from heaven, as of a rushing mighty wind, and it filled the whole house where they were sitting. ³ Then there appeared to them divided tongues, as of fire, and one sat upon each of them. ⁴ And they were all **filled with the Holy Spirit** and began to speak with other tongues, as the Spirit gave them utterance."* Acts 2:1-4

I rely on the Holy Spirit to get through life. When I was going through my darkest moments, it was the Holy Spirit who directed me to stay connected to God, to play the Word of God when I couldn't read it. It was the Holy Spirit who directed me to saturate the atmosphere of my home with worship music, even when I wasn't home. It was the Holy Spirt who was whispering in my ear not to give up, but to keep trusting God. The Holy Spirit is real, and He is waiting for you to acknowledge Him and invite Him into your everyday life.

It is my mission to make sure the Holy Spirit gets the recognition, love, respect, and reverence that He so richly deserves. I think it will help the Body of Christ to develop that appreciation if they do a study on the Holy Spirt and learn about His character and how He functions.

The beautiful thing about the Holy Spirit is that according to 1 Corinthians 6:19-20, if you are a Believer in Jesus Christ, He already abides inside of you. The Bible goes on to say that our bodies are not our own for we were bought at a price, and what is that price? The precious Blood of Jesus. But unfortunately, many Believers do not realize that He is abiding in them, nor do they understand that they have access to Him 24/7.

The Holy Spirit is often silent. He does not give unsolicited advice. The Holy Spirit is a complete gentleman. He does not enter your life unless invited to do so. He gently imparts, directs, and teaches. That's why it's so important to keep an intimate relationship with Him. Because of His gentle nature, you can easily miss His gentle probing. Here are some of His attributes that we often overlook:

1) The Holy Spirit feels, thinks, and wills.
2) The Holy Spirit has all the divine attributes: Omniscient, Omnipresent, and Omnipotent.
3) The Holy Spirit speaks only the truth.
4) The Holy Spirit is wise.
5) The Holy Spirit is a teacher of truth.

I am a living witness that you can avoid so many mistakes by listening to the Holy Spirit's direction. I can remember a time when I woke up and could barely walk. I thought a disc had slipped in my back, so I called my chiropractor. He advised that it probably wasn't anything serious and to just ice/heat my back and lay down. But the Holy Spirit led me to call another doctor who advised that I go to the hospital.

In pain, I drove myself to the ER and they detected that I was septic. Had I taken the advice of my chiropractor and stayed home, I would have eventually died. But God wasn't finished with me yet! Every time I think about it, I praise God for the Holy Spirit directing me that day.

While going through the wilderness, I not only felt disconnected with God the Father, but I also felt disconnected from the Holy Spirit. I was not as sensitive to His gentle nudging as I had once been. I could not always detect His voice from my own, so I found myself in situations that I could have avoided if I had been obedient to the Holy Spirit directing me another way.

There were times when the Lord would bless me with finances, but not being in tune with the Holy Spirit and seeking His wisdom, as fast as the money came in, it would go out. I listed earlier that one of the Holy Spirit's characteristics is that He is omnipresent. He was always right there with me in the wilderness, yet I did not cling to Him and seek His direction. I am so glad that He never gave up on me and continued to guide me through the wilderness until I saw the light of day. I have clung to Him tightly ever since.

Some may ask, "How do you hear the Holy Spirit's voice?" First, you must invite Him into your life, and second, you must develop a relationship with Him. The *"still small voice"* mentioned in I Kings 19:11 is how the Holy Spirit speaks to us today.

If you have not invited the Holy Spirit into your life, please do so immediately. He's not some kind of mystical character. He's a part of the Holy Trinity: the Father, the Son, and the Holy Spirit. He is real, and He will make a real difference in your life if you let Him.

The lyrics to this song by Kim Walker say it all:

Holy Spirit

There's nothing worth more, that will ever come close
No thing can compare, You're our living hope
Your Presence
I've tasted and seen, of the sweetest of Loves
Where my heart becomes free, and my shame is undone
In Your Presence
Holy Spirit You are welcome here
Come flood this place and fill the atmosphere
Your Glory God is what our hearts long for
To be overcome by Your Presence Lord
Let us become more aware of Your Presence
Let us experience the Glory of Your Goodness
Holy Spirit You are welcome here
Come flood this place and fill the atmosphere
Your Glory God is what our hearts long for
To be overcome by Your Presence Lord

Source: LyricFind
Holy Spirit lyrics © Capitol Christian Music Group S Featuring Artist: Kim Walker-Smith

Principle #5 - Acknowledge His Deity [Lordship]

*"But **the LORD** is the **true** God, **He** is the **living God**, and an everlasting King: At His wrath the earth quakes, and the nations cannot endure His indignation."*

Jeremiah 10:10 [ESV]

"For in Christ all the fullness of the Deity lives in bodily form…"

Colossians 2:9 [NIV]

Definition: **de·i·ty** - one exalted or revered as supremely good or powerful

God is a Sovereign God. The Easton Bible Dictionary defines God's Sovereignty as "His absolute right to do all things according to His own good pleasure." One of God's redemptive names that describes His Deity is El Elyon—He is the Most-High God.

God said to Moses, "I AM WHO I AM." And this is what you are to say to the Israelites: "'I Am' has sent me to you" (see Exodus 3:14). If we want to maintain a personal relationship with Him, the fact that He is a sovereign God, that He is the great I Am and He is GOD all by Himself, should give us great comfort, especially in times of uncertainty.

Between the years 2018–2021, I experienced one of the driest seasons of my Christian life. I often felt disappointed with the hand life had dealt me and often in despair, yet I always reflected on God's sovereignty. There was always that still small voice inside that would not and could not let me give up on God, because I knew He was my only hope, my only solution to getting out of that weary wilderness.

Acknowledging God's Deity is so important because it establishes that He has the supreme power, that He is the key to getting through any dry season you will ever find yourself in. We must declare, "at the name of Jesus **every knee should bow, of things in heaven, and things in earth, and things under the earth**; and that every tongue should confess that Jesus Christ is Lord, to the glory of God the Father" Philippians 2:10-11.

In the book of Job, after suffering many tremendous losses, Job's friends begin to question God, and although the priest Elihu tries to defend God and shares with Job who God really is, God Himself thought it best that He addressed Job directly.

"Then the LORD answered Job out of the whirlwind and said:

"Who is this that darkens counsel by words without knowledge? Dress for action like a man; I will question you, and you make it known to Me.

"Where were you when I laid the foundation of the earth? Tell Me, if you have understanding

"Or who shut in the sea with doors when it burst out from the womb…

"Have you commanded the morning since your days began, and caused the dawn to know its place? Have you comprehended the expanse of the earth? Declare, if you know all this.

"Have you entered the storehouses of the snow, or have you seen the storehouses of the hail?..." Job 38 (ESV)

In these passages, God tore down any arguments about His authority and put things back into prospective. HE IS GOD—period, end of discussion. He is not some mystical myth; He is Jehovah, El Shaddai, Lord God Almighty.

There will be times when we may question why God allowed certain tragedies to occur in our lives. We may even be mad at Him for a season, but I do not think it's a wise thing to confront God regarding His Deity, because He will win every time!

When I was going through my lowest times, I got on my knees and began to weep before God, and I said to Him, "How dare I ask You for anything when I can't even give You my undivided attention? You (God) deserve better. You deserve more. It's because of You that I am alive, and it's because of You that I survived sepsis. It's because of You that I have a job. It's because of You that I have a home, and You deserve more. You deserve better."

It was during this time that I came to the stark realization that He is God and all power is in His hands. It's in those *"what is man that You are mindful of him, and the son of man that You care for him?"* [Psalm 8:4] moments that I acknowledge His preeminence in my life and allow Him to sit on the throne of my heart.

I often sing this song to the Lord just to affirm to Him that I recognize His Deity:

"There's only one word to describe
And only one word comes to mind
There's only one word to describe
Holy, Holy, Lord God Almighty
Holy, Holy, Lord God Almighty
There is no one like You
You are Holy"

Holy by Jesus Culture – Consumed Album 2009

To give you a head start, here are some scriptures regarding God's Deity:

- *"See now that I am* **He***;* **there is no God besides** *Me. I bring death and I give* **life***; I wound and I heal, and* **there is no one who** *can deliver from My hand."* Isiah 45:51

- *But* **the LORD** *is the* **true** *God,* **He** *is the* **living God***, and an everlasting king: At his wrath the earth quakes, and the nations cannot endure his indignation."* Jeremiah 10:10 [ESV]

- *"And we know that the Son of God has come and has given us understanding, so that we may know Him who is true; and we are in Him who is true, in His Son Jesus Christ. He is the true God and eternal life."* I John 5:20 [ESV]

- *"And I heard every creature in heaven and on earth and under the earth and in the sea, and all that is in them, saying, "To Him who sits on the throne and to the Lamb be blessing and honor and glory and might forever and ever!"* Rev 5:13 [NIV]

Principle #6 - Tell Him You Love Him often

*"...I thirst with the deepest longings to **love** You more..."*
Psalm 63:1 (Passion)

Definition: **love** - strong affection for another arising out of kinship or personal ties

Loving God is both an honor and a privilege. He has already proven His love for us. He paid the ultimate price by allowing His only begotten Son to be crucified on our behalf so that we might have a right to an abundant life, miss hell, and make heaven our home. But how do we, the benefactors of this great sacrifice, in turn show our love toward Him (see Psalm 116:12)?

Remember when I shared about Vertical Worship being an intimate relationship between you and God? Well, that was the start. Love is birthed out of intimacy, and that intimacy is built on words of adoration and affirmation. Love can only be given to someone you have established a personal relationship with, and the way you do that is by spending time with that person. Get to know them so you can understand them, know what brings them joy, and then do the thing that brings them joy. It's taking the time to talk with them and understand their heart toward the many issues of life.

I can truly say that I have developed that personal relationship with God. God and I go way back—all the way back to before I was in my mother's womb—where He saw me, knew me, and set me apart (Jeremiah 5:1). But unfortunately, I can only go back as far as 1981, when I accepted Him as my personal Savior. But ever since then, I have discovered more and more about my Savior. I developed a thirst for Him that cannot be quenched by food, drugs, or sex. It can't be quenched by dancing, doing good deeds, or even sharing the gospel. This particular thirst can ONLY be quenched by spending time with Him—by totally surrendering to Him and falling in love with Him more and more each day.

What do we do as humans when we fall in love with someone? We write love letters, perform acts of kindness, pay attention to what they like and surprise them, and most importantly, we tell them that we love them. There is nothing that can take the place of the spoken word.

I never actually fell in love until I was saved. I had a few boyfriends in high school and college and have been engaged twice, but once the relationship was over, it was over—there was no real love lost. I was beginning to wonder if I even had a heart! It was when I first got saved that my heart began to soften. I was so into God that I didn't think about dating for a while. I was so wonderfully and uttering in love with Him that I didn't even miss my relationships with a man.

After a while, I let down my guard and opened my heart to love. It was my involvement with my first boyfriend after I was saved that made me realize I really did have a heart, and I gave it all I had. I thought that since we had been saved, this relationship would be different because we both loved the Lord.

But as life would have it, we broke up a year later and I was devastated. I went to bed crying, woke up crying, walked to work crying, and had to go to the bathroom at work crying. I prayed, "Lord, please make it stop. Please ease the pain." It took months, but finally the pain subsided.

This was around the same time when I was introduced to worship music and left the Pentecostal church and started attending a non-denomination church. So there I was, in a new environment, experiencing a new style of worship, and my heart was aching. I would often say to the Lord, "If I could only be happy for happiness' sake, not because a **man** makes me happy, but because **You** make me happy."

One day, I heard someone teaching about the difference between the words "happy" and "joy." The teacher said happiness was based on a "happening." If something happens, it can bring me happiness, but something else can bring me sadness. Whereas joy was more intrinsic, developed from within and not based on a happening.

As I am writing this, I found this quote from a PositivelyJane blog that sums it up: *"Joy is in the heart. Happiness is on the face. Joy is of the soul. Happiness is of the moment."*

It was around this time in my life that I realized how much I loved the Lord and that I could not rely on another human to bring me joy like the Lord could. Another person can enhance my happiness, but only the Lord and bring me pure, sustaining joy. It was this revelation, coupled with the scripture, *"The joy of the Lord is my strength"* (Nehemiah 8:10), that solidified my utter dependance on the Lord. I was hooked.

During the driest seasons of my life, I never ceased to tell the Lord I loved Him. I would wake up most mornings saying, "I love You, Lord; I love you, Jesus; I love you, Holy Spirit." Even though life prevented me from spending quality time with the Lord, I would always let Him know that I loved Him. I had to develop my own love language when interacting with the Lord.

The Bible says that we should love the Lord because He first loved us. This is true because I would have never known what real love was if God hadn't first displayed His love toward me. I first started to love God out of obligation or command by scripture, but then I began to genuinely love Him. Not because I was commanded to do so, but because I wanted to. I was no longer obligated to love Him; I now loved Him out of relationship. I was hopelessly and wonderfully in love with Him. I began to love Him for WHO He is and not WHAT He can do for me. I began to feel that "as the deer pants for the water, so my soul longs after you" type of love. And now that I have experienced this love for the Lord and am able to reciprocate His love, I wouldn't trade it for the world.

When you are in the wilderness, you have to keep proclaiming your love for the Lord. Proclaim who He is whether you feel it or not, because it's not about emotions; it's about proclaiming the truth.

You might not feel it at first, but proclaim it until you do. That's how you survive in the wilderness. Proclaim what you know to be true about the Lord.

Revelation 2:5 gives us instruction on what we should do when we find ourselves in a season when we feel isolated from the Lord: "Remember therefore *from* whence thou art fallen, and repent, and do the *first works*;". (KJV) So I humbled myself, laid out before the Lord, and repented for my many inconsistencies concerning Him. Then I went back to my first Love.

I began to listen to songs like "Purify My Heart" and repeated back to the Lord what the psalmist was improvising. I told Him, "I want my heart to become Your home. Take up residence in my Heart." And then I took hold of this scripture and made it my own: "**One thing** have I **desired of the LORD**, that will I seek after; that I may dwell in the house of the **LORD** all the days of my life, to behold the beauty." Psalm 27:4

There is nothing more fulfilling or rewarding than loving God and worshiping Him out of a real love relationship. If you have never experienced this type of relationship with the Lord, I encourage you to start now, today. Wherever you are, lift your eyes, your hands, your heart—whatever you can lift—and let the Lord know that you want to get closer to Him, that you want to experience a real love relationship with Him. He is right there waiting, and He will move right into those empty spaces in your heart and flood you with a love so awesome that you won't be able to do anything else but reciprocate.

Below are some additional scriptures on loving God. My prayer is that they will minister to your heart and spark that love for God that is deep within you.

- ❖ I love you, O LORD, my strength. The LORD is my rock and my fortress and my deliverer, my rock, in whom I take refuge, my shield, and the horn of my salvation, my stronghold." Psalm 18:1- 3

- ❖ "I love the LORD, because He has heard my voice and my pleas for mercy. Because He inclined His ear to me, therefore I will call on Him as long as I live." Psalm 116:1

- ❖ "Now, Israel, what does the Lord your God require from you, but to fear the Lord your God, to walk in all His ways **and love Him,** and to serve the Lord your God with all your heart and with all your soul," Deuteronomy 10:12

- ❖ "…by **loving the Lord your God**, by obeying His voice, and by holding fast to Him; for this is your life and the length of your days, that you may live in the land which the Lord swore to your fathers," Deuteronomy 30:20

- ❖ "…and **you shall love** the Lord your God with all your heart, and with all your soul, and with all your mind, and with all your strength." Mark 12:30 (similar scripture in Deuteronomy, Matthew, and Luke)

Principle #7 - Sing Love Songs to Him

*"I sing through the night under your splendor-shadow, offering up to you my **songs** of delight and joy!"* Psalm 63:7 [TPT]

Definition: **sing** – to make musical sounds with the voice, especially words with a set tune

"I love you, Lord, and I lift my voice; to worship You, oh my soul rejoices. Take joy, my King, in what you hear; let it be a sweet, sweet sound in Your ear." This is one of the most popular love songs you can sing to the Lord. It's short, sweet, and to the point.

Once you establish a loving relationship with the Lord as we discussed in the previous chapter, the next thing you may start doing is singing to the Lord. I am not talking about the congregational singing that you do at church; no, this will come from a deeper place in your heart. It will feel like a well of water springing up out of your soul.

In my quest to maintain intimacy with the Lord, I created CDs (I am dating myself again here. Now they are called "Playlists") filled with worship songs geared toward building up my love relationship with the Lord. The more I sing to Him, the more I fall in love with Him. The more I fall in love with Him, the more I want to be in His Presence. And the more I stay in His Presence, the more I am changed.

Singing is another way of making confessions or declarations. It's speaking into the atmosphere and ultimately changing it. When you sing, it first affects you, then the one to whom you are singing.

I must warn you that you should be in agreement with what you are singing. If it is a song about the greatness of God, then you are declaring how great God is. If it is a song about Holiness, you are declaring the Holiness of God into the atmosphere. If it is a song about loving God, you are declaring openly and unashamedly how much you love the Lord.

I would like to take a break here and share a bit on singing songs on the topic of surrender. There are a lot of songs out there that talk about surrender, and I want to admonish you to understand the lyrics before you make the declaration of your undying surrender to God, for you may be making a commitment you are not ready to keep. To be quite honest with you, most of us are only partially surrendered and have a long way to go before we can declare our whole surrender to God. Total surrender is a tremendous step; it takes a fully consecrated life and dying to self.

Instead, I encourage you to seek God and tell Him exactly how you feel. Let Him know that you want to be totally surrendered to Him but are struggling with letting go of some areas of your life. The struggle is real; believe me, I know it all too well. It's part of our spiritual growth. The Lord wants to hear from you. He wants you to be open and honest with Him, and you will get there, I promise.

James 5:13 NIV says, "Is anyone among you in trouble? Let them pray. Is anyone happy? Let them sing songs of praise." During my time in the wilderness or even during my times of struggle, it was crucial that I kept my communication lines open with the Lord, and one of the major ways I did that was by singing to Him. Now that I've come through the wilderness, I still sing to the Lord. I can listen to a ton of worship songs, but it's not until I sing the song myself that I am fully engaged in worship. When I was struggling to get into His presence, I not only listened to love songs, but I found that when I sang the love songs to Him directly, I was truly worshiping Him. And what I love about it is that you don't have to know HOW to sing. This is not a contest where you will be judged on your vocal ability—God is not a judge on *The Voice*. God is only looking at your heart, and I am so glad about that!

As you sing, it should resonate with your spirit. The words you are singing let the whole spiritual world know—especially the Lord—how you really feel about Him. Listen to the words of this song and see if it matches how you feel about your Lord:

Lord, You are more Precious than silver
Lord, You are more costly than gold
Lord, You are more beautiful than diamonds, and
nothing I desire compares with You
Artist: Jason Wright Album: Heavenward

This song lets the Lord know how precious He is to me. I do not normally talk like this, but this songwriter was able to put together some beautiful words which allow me to express some deeper feelings I have toward the Lord.

When I sing this song, I am saying, "Lord, I know that silver and gold are precious metals and that diamonds are beautiful gemstones, and very expensive. But none of these expensive things can be compared to You, because You are more precious, more costly, and more beautiful than them all."

Singing is a powerful mode of expression. Do not allow the enemy to silence your worship through song to your King of Kings. Telling the LORD that you love Him is a powerful declaration, but singing Him love songs is a whole other realm of declaring your unfaltering love for Him.

Here is a song that best describes how I feel about the Lord.:

"There is none like You
No one else can touch my heart like You do
And I could search for all eternity, Lord
And find, there is none like You"

There is None like You
Originally by Lenny Leblanc
Song by Don Moen and Paul Wilbur Heal Our Land Album 2013

Singing to the Lord really enhances your worship experience. If you are looking to grow your relationship with the Lord or if you are going through a dry season in which you feel far away from Him, I would challenge you to add singing to your devotional time with Him. Or better yet, sing to Him extemporaneously, or while you are driving, and watch how you will begin to soar in the spirit.

Principle #8 - Develop a Lasting Friendship with Him

"Some friendships don't last for long, but there is one loving friend who is joined to your heart closer than any other!
Proverbs 18:1 [TPT]

Definition: **friend** · 1. a person known well to another and regarded with liking, affection, and loyalty; an intimate · 2. an acquaintance or associate · 3. an ally in a fight

I have lived in three states over the span of sixty years, and I can honestly say that I have established some solid relationships in all three of those states. In the New York/New Jersey area, I have at least six solid relationships that I have maintained over the last thirty-seven years. And I have established more than that in my twenty years living in Texas.

I truly believe that the secret to a long-lasting friendship is mutual respect. A friend is someone you can depend on to be there during the tough seasons of your life. A friend is someone you can wake up at two a.m. and they will jump in their car and come over to hold your hand during a time of a tragedy. A true friend knows you intimately, meaning that you have a close personal relationship that is hard to break. They share your secrets.

In church, we often speak about God as being our Lord, our Savior, our Protector, and our Healer, and so He is, but you don't hear the Saints often speak about God as their friend. Maybe because we think He is too high above us, and He is. Or that He doesn't have time to be friends with His creations because He's too busy listening to our prayers and giving us guidance. But truth be told, God wants to be our Friend as well as our Lord and Savior.

In James 2:23, we learn that "Abraham believed God, and it was counted to him as righteousness—and he was called a friend of God."

We as believers not only have to cultivate our love relationship with the Lord, but we must also cultivate our friendship as well. Talk to Him like you would a best friend—your spiritual best friend. Share secrets with Him; share things you wouldn't share with other people. He is the most loyal, loving, and dependable friend you will ever have. Your secrets are safe with Him. You will never have to worry about hearing about something you shared in confidentiality exploited on Facebook or Instagram.

During my loneliest times, I have grown closer to the Lord as a Friend. He understands me. He knows me and, most importantly, He wants the best for me. I can share my innermost thoughts with Him without the fear of being judged, ridiculed, or ostracized. I can be completely honest with Him and know that He doesn't think I'm the "weird child." I can be still with Him for hours and just purely enjoy His company. When I am going through something and NEED my friend, I cut off the music and put away my phone. I don't want to check the latest tweets on Twitter, or the latest post on Facebook. I don't want to look at the videos on Instagram. I want to give Him my undivided attention and pour out my heart to Him and allow Him to pour His wisdom back into me. And when we are finished meeting, I don't need to post on Facebook what an awesome experience we had. I don't have to create a Facebook story about what was said because what we shared was so intimate, so personal, and it was just between the two of us. And that's enough for me.

Proverbs 18:24 says, "But there is a friend that **sticketh closer than a brother**." There is no distance between true friends, so if you have one, hold on to them because they are rare and very hard to come by.

According to Wikipedia, "Friendship is a relationship of mutual affection between people. It is a stronger form of interpersonal bond than an acquaintance." Use this definition as a barometer of where you are in your relationship with the Lord. Is He just Lord of your life, the One who has forgiven your sin, or is He both Lord and a Friend in your life? Is there a mutual affection between you and the Lord? Or is your relationship just a mere acquaintance? Nothing can top being Lord, Master, and Savior, but it's the friendship factor that helps develop intimacy with God.

Principle #9 - Don't Isolate Yourself

"An unfriendly person isolates himself and seems to care only about his own issues." Proverbs 18:1 [TPT]

Definition: **i·so·late** - cause (a person or place) to be or remain alone or apart from others.

If you are going through a wilderness experience, please don't isolate yourself. I know this sounds like an oxymoron. You are probably asking, "How can I not be isolated when I'm in the middle of the wilderness and I feel like no one is around?" And this is true; it's in the wilderness when you feel very much alone and isolated. But please do not **intentionally isolate** yourself. Have you ever heard people say they feel alone in a crowded room? I think that occurs when people are feeling so isolated that it doesn't matter whether people are around. The person may be feeling such despair that they are in their own little world looking out at the rest of society. If you are feeling this level of isolation, please speak to someone who can help you out of that dark space.

When I talk about not isolating yourself while in the wilderness, I mean don't cut off all matter of communication with others and feel like you have to go through it alone. The enemy can use isolation as a tactic to make you feel like you are all by yourself and nobody understands what you are going through. We need each other in the Body of Christ. We all have a unique gift that we bring to the Body, and we need to share it with others. The Word of God says that we should encourage one another and build one another up (I Thessalonians 5:11).

Consider solitary confinement in the prison system. Prisoners are placed in a cell by themselves as punishment to mentally break them down. It is also known as segregation, restrictive housing, lockdown, and isolation. During their stay in solitary confinement, the prisoner has no cell phone, no laptop, and no TV. They have no visitors or witty conversations. They may have a small window that allows some daylight to shine through, but that's it. They eat, sleep, and poop in the same room for days on end. The only contact they have with other humans is for maybe an hour a day to get some exercise and eat. Instead of disciplining the inmate, however, this type of confinement can lead to depression, hallucinations, panic attacks, and suicide.

The pandemic was a form of solitary confinement, especially for those who lived alone. But one major difference (besides not being sentenced) is that we had the option of communicating with others via Facebook, Teams, Zoom, Face Time, and let's not forget the good old-fashioned telephone. There are so many other technological ways to stay in touch, but to many, that still wasn't enough because it couldn't take the place of human touch.

We all need to be alone sometimes. It's actually good to be alone to write down your thoughts, meditate on the Word, study, and most importantly to communicate with God. While there are seasons of aloneness, it shouldn't go on for long periods of time. The human psyche is more delicate than we think it is. Traumatic experiences and long periods of isolation can break a person's will.

It is not God's original design to be alone. He even declared it in Genesis 2:18-25 when He said, "It is not good for the man to be alone. I will make a helper suitable for him." So He created the woman, and wasn't that a glorious day?

It's the enemy's tactic to isolate you in times of trouble. That's one of the reasons why God said in Psalm 133:1 that it was "good to fellowship one with another." We need supportive relationships in our lives. Did you ever wonder where that old expression "no man is an island" comes from? Back in 1623, an English poet by the name of John Donne coined this phrase when he was seriously ill during the winter. The basis of what he was expressing is that no one is self-sufficient; everyone relies on others somehow. He believed that we all must depend on someone else at some point in order to survive. Can you imagine him on his sick bed in the dead of winter? He may have had a fever or perhaps he was bedridden. If so, he would have needed someone to hand him a glass of water, give him his medicine, or help him to the bathroom—or more graphically, change his bedpan.

In this season of my life, I am a single woman and I live alone. I thoroughly enjoy my own company and like being alone at times. But when I am not feeling good or have a fever, all I want to do is crawl into bed and have someone make me a cup of tea or a bowl of soup. I vividly remember when I woke up one morning and could not walk out of my house to get into my car. I had to call my manager to come from work to help me down the steps and into my car. At that point, living alone was a scary time in my life.

Isolation is not necessarily a bad thing, but you must not stay there too long. Humans are social beings. We thrive on relationships with others. God designed us that way. We were not only made to worship God, but also to interact with others.

Hezekiah Walker said it best in his song "I Need You to Survive:"

I need you, you need me
We're all a part of God's body
Stand with me, agree with me
We're all a part of God's body
It is His will, that every need be supplied
You are important to me, I need you to survive
You are important to me, I need you to survive

By Hezekiah Walker & LFC – Family Affair II Life at Radio City Music Hall

Isolation in itself is not necessarily a bad thing, but you shouldn't stay there too long. Human beings are social beings. We thrive on relationships with others. God designed us that way. We were not only made to worship God; we were also made to interact with others.

Here are some additional scriptures on the importance of needing others:

- ❖ *"And let us consider how to stir up one another to love and good works."* Hebrews 10:24

- ❖ *"...not neglecting to meet together, as is the habit of some, but encouraging one another, and all the more as you see the Day drawing near."* Hebrews 10:25
- ❖ *"Two are better than one, because they have a good reward for their toil. For if they fall, one will lift up his fellow. But woe to him who is alone when he falls and has not another to lift him up! Again, if two lie together, they keep warm, but how can one keep warm alone? And though a man might prevail against one who is alone, two will withstand him—a threefold cord is not quickly broken."* Ecclesiastes 4:9-12
- ❖ *"Iron sharpens iron, and one man sharpens another." Proverbs 27:17*
- ❖ *"For where two or three are gathered in my name, there am I among them."* Matthew 18:20
- ❖ *"Bear one another's burdens, and so fulfill the law of Christ."* Galatians 6:2

Principle #10 - Bathe Yourself in the Word of God

"Thy word have I hid in mine heart, That I might not sin against Thee." Psalm 119:11 [KJV]

Definition: **the Word of God** – 1. refers to God's own speech as He brings order out of chaos and makes His will known. 2. The bible 3. God's love letter to mankind

The Word of God is the most important thing in the life of the Believer. It is vital to our existence. With it, we live. Without it, we die. Need I say more? God's Word, also known as the Bible or the Sword of the Spirit, is our instruction manual. It sustains us. It guides us. It heals us and it leads us into victory.

According to Hebrews 4:12, *"the Word of God is alive and active. Sharper than any double-edged sword, it penetrates even to dividing soul and spirit, joints and marrow; it judges the thoughts and attitudes of the heart."* This confirms both the power and the weigh that the Word of God carries.

My pastor starts every message by saying, "The people of God live in front of the Word of God," and I totally agree with him. In order to live out this Christian walk, we must keep the Word of God before us, because everything we need to live a victorious, peaceful, prosperous and health life can be found in within the pages of the Word. We learn how to conduct ourselves in business, how to live holy, how to treat others, how to rebuke the enemy, and how to maintain our sanity.

It takes time to read the Word. You have to not only read it, but you have to digest it, meditate on it. Then you have to apply it to your life on a daily basis. Unfortunately, the average Christian does not realize the importance that the Word of God holds in their lives. We, and I am including myself, allow the cares of this world to come between us and our Bible. We get busy with raising our families, trying to succeed at our jobs or businesses, continuing our education and just living life. It's easy to move the Word of God further and further out of our lives. It starts off with missing a day, then a week, then a month, and if we are not careful, we can go months without evening picking up our Bible.

The problem is, the further we move away from the Word of God, the more we begin to die a slow death spiritually. Job said, *"I have treasured the **words of His mouth** more than my necessary food...* (Job 23:12)." I like how the amplified version puts it: "I have **esteemed** and **treasured** the words of His mouth."

Job came to the realization that he had more respect and placed more value on the Word of God than he had for natural food. He realized he needed the Word of God in order to sustain himself spiritually.

Like Job, we must feed our spirits with the Word of God, otherwise we will not grow spiritually. And if we don't grow spiritually, the passion for God will gradually fade.

I knew all of this, yet I still allowed myself to drift away from the Word. I did not read the Word of God nearly as much as I needed in order to sustain my spiritual growth. This is when I knew that I was entering into a wilderness experience. I loved the Lord with all my heart, mind, and soul. I trusted Him with my life. I tried to live my life in a manner that would be pleasing in His sight. He was always the deciding factor in my life, and I knew I was nothing—absolutely nothing—without him, yet I had become so casual with His Word.

There's something about going through a wilderness experience that knocks all the good sense the Lord gave you right out of you. I became that girl—the one who professes Christianity, but not necessarily equipping myself to be a successful Christian. Me—the one who is always quoting scriptures. I must have over three dozen scriptures in this book alone, yet I had lost my momentum to study the Word of God for myself. I often felt like Apostle Paul in the book of Romans 7:15-20; "I do not understand what I do. For what I want to do I do not do, but what I hate I do."

When I first accepted Jesus Christ as my Lord and Savior back in 1981, I drank, ate, and digested the Word of God. I am an avid note taker, and I would come home from church and pull out the major points of the sermon and plaster them all over my walls. I would type confessions from the Word of God and make posters. I learned to quote the Word, proclaim the promises of God through the Word, and even fight the enemy with the Word of God. Yes, I learned early that the Word of God was to be the number one thing to sustain me throughout my walk with the Lord.

I sincerely believe that memorizing the Word of God in my earlier years sustained me during my time in the wilderness, and still sustains me to this day. For when I pray, the Holy Spirit brings scriptures back to my remembrance that pertain to the exact thing I am praying about. This lets me know that the Word still resides inside me and that it still works! It never loses its potency.

I sincerely believe that memorizing the Word of God in my earlier years was the thing that sustained me during my time in the wilderness, and still sustains me to this day. For when I pray, the Holy Spirit would begin to bring scriptures back to my memory that pertains to the exact thing we are praying about. This lets me know that it is still inside me and that the Word still works! It never loses its potency.

The Lord in His infinite wisdom made it possible to have the Word of God converted onto various technical devices. There is the Bible on CD, DVD, electronic devices, YouTube, and Kindle. You can even download the Bible app onto your cell phone. We are literally without excuse. *I* was without excuse.

Yet I still lost my passion and my drive to study the Word. Here I was in the wilderness and literally not engaging in the Word on a daily basis. Thank God for the Holy Spirit that I had just enough sense to put myself on life support. If I wasn't reading the Bible, I would listen to the Word of God. I purchased the CDs and downloaded the Bible to my Kindle and cell phone.

But unfortunately, I still wasn't consistent in listening to the Word every day. What was the matter with me? I had to ask myself, "Do you want to die here in this wilderness?" I had come so far. The Lord had given me so many lifelines. I was getting to know Him more, I was loving on Him, singing love songs to Him. I was developing a friendship with Him, not isolating myself and allowing the Holy Spirit to guide and direct me, yet this had become the biggest hurdle for me to overcome if I was to ever get out of this dry season.

I felt both defeated and deflated. I was dying a slow death spiritually and did not know what to do about it. I had two choices: I could be like the children of Israel and murmur, complain, and wander around the wilderness for another forty years, or I could take this major lifeline—this literal manna from Heaven—and stand on the Word of God and allow it to guide me to the promise land. I chose the latter.

The words of an old hymn came to mind: "On Christ the solid rock I stand, all other ground is sinking sand." Once again, the Lord gave me a lifeline—and it was Him Himself. He took me back to my first love. I had to eat and drink the Word of God like I used to when I was first saved.

Then Galatians 2:20 came to life in my heart again: *"**I have been crucified with Christ and I no longer live, but Christ lives in me**.*

The life I live in the body, I live by faith in the Son of God, who loved me and gave Himself for me. I do not set aside the grace of God, for if righteousness could be gained through the law, Christ died for nothing!"

I had to learn, and am still learning, how to balance this thing called life. I had to come to the end of myself, realizing I cannot do it all, and lean more on the Lord. I had to meditate on that scripture that says, "The life I live in the body, I live by faith in the Son of God, who loved me and gave Himself for me." This was life-changing for me. Jesus Christ gave Himself for me so that I would have a right to the tree of life, but also so that I could live by faith in the Son of God. If I really believe that Jesus gave Himself for me, I need to show my appreciation and give all of myself to Him. In order to do that, I need to get to know Him through His word. He knew life would be hard here on earth when He left, so He gave us a lifeline called the Word of God. He knew we would have dry seasons and would need to drink from the Word of God, that we would have times of doubt and unbelief and would need to receive comfort from the Word of God. He knew there would come a time when we would be so hungry for the truth and would need to eat the word of God.

I consider the Bible to be God's love letter to mankind. In it, not only does He give us instructions on how to live, but He also shares His incredible, never-ending passionate love toward us. If any of you have ever been in love, you know what it is like to receive a love letter from the one you love. You read it over and over again, look forward to receiving it, read every word, and you cherish it. And if your love is a distant one, you probably have a special place where you place your letters so you can treasure them for years to come. That is how we ought to feel about the Word of God, and that's how I felt about the Word of God in the beginning. Now I had rekindled that passion once again.

I won't sit here and say that after that prayer, everything miraculously changed. I didn't suddenly become a Bible scholar or even revert to some of my old ways. But one thing is abundantly clear: I needed God and His God's Word, and it helped me make it out of my wilderness experience.

If you have been struggling to get into your bible, here are some more scriptures to show the importance of the Word of God:

- ❖ *"All scripture is given by inspiration of God, and is profitable for doctrine, for reproof, for correction, for instruction in righteousness."* 2 Timothy 3:16
- ❖ *"Every word of God proves true; He is a shield to those who take refuge in Him."* Proverbs 30:5
- ❖ *"The unfolding of Your words gives light; it imparts understanding to the simple."* Psalm 119:130
- ❖ *"How can a young person stay on the path of purity? By living according to Your word. I seek You with all my heart; do not let me stray from Your commands."* Psalm 119:9-10

- ❖ *"For as the rain and the snow come down from heaven and do not return there but water the earth, making it bring forth and sprout, giving seed to the sower and bread to the eater, so shall My word be that goes out from my mouth; it shall not return to me empty, but it shall accomplish that which I purpose, and shall succeed in the thing for which I sent it."* Isaiah 55:10-11
- ❖ *"Heaven and earth will disappear, but My words will never disappear."* Matthew 24:35
- ❖ *"Grass dries up, and flowers wither, but our God's word will last forever."* Isaiah 40:8
- ❖ *"For My thoughts are not Your thoughts, neither are your ways My ways, declares the Lord."* Isaiah 55:8

"A thorough knowledge of the Bible is worth more than a college education." Theodore Roosevelt

Principle #11 - Exercise – Start Moving!

"For physical training is of some value, but godliness has value for all things, holding promise for both the present life and the life to come." 1 Timothy 4:8 [NIV]

Definition: **ex·er·cise** - activity requiring physical effort, carried out to sustain or improve health and fitness

According to Mayo Clinic, "Exercise helps prevent and improve a number of health problems, including high blood pressure, diabetes, and arthritis. Research on depression, anxiety, and exercise shows that the psychological and physical benefits of exercise can also help improve mood and reduce anxiety. Exercising releases endorphins, which are feel-good brain chemicals that can enhance your sense of well-being."

When you are in a dry season, your body is depleted of some necessary nutrients. You're both hot and thirsty and nothing can quench that thirst like water. But because your body is depleted, you feel tired and sluggish and all you want to do is sleep. Exercise is the last thing on your mind. There was many a day that I looked past my squat machine, walked past my elliptical glider, and went to bed. I wanted to exercise because I needed to lose weight for health purposes, but I didn't feel like exercising because I had lost all drive and motivation.

I am so glad the Lord saw the cry of my heart and helped me to rise up from that dry and miserable place and gave me back the strength to get back into an exercise routine. Praise God! When I took that first step, the endorphins were released and I had a burst of energy that I had not experienced in a long time. After a while, I noticed that I was beginning to shed a few pounds without even trying this time. This was another answer to my prayers.

After my energy returned so I could exercise, I also received the motivation to get up early to meet with the Lord. It's amazing how the Lord will honor your unspoken requests. For years, it had been my heart's desire to get up and spend time with the Lord before I got ready for work—every day, not just on the weekends. But as much as my spirit was willing, my flesh was weak and every time the alarm went off, I would just roll over and go back to sleep.

But then one day, my clock went off at five a.m. and instead of hitting the snooze bar, I leaped out of bed and on my knees with great anticipation to meet with the Lord in the quiet hours of the morning. Now I was not only exercising my natural body; I was also exercising my spiritual body again.

The Lord had revealed another characteristic of Himself to me. In this moment, He revealed Himself as Jehovah Roi—the Lord who sees me. Who would have thought that a simple thing like exercise could lead me into a deeper relationship with the Lord? That is just one of the reasons I love Him so much. He is so concerned with every aspect of our lives.

If you are not incorporating exercise into your daily life, I encourage you to start doing so. As we get older, we start to slow down. We have to remember We are a spirit; we possess a soul and live in a body. No matter how much we may soar in spirit, if our bodies are not in shape, it can be a major hinderance to our overall growth and development. Simple things like stretching and movement will get those endorphins moving and get us up and out to do the work of the Lord.

*"Do you not know that in a race all the runners run, but only one gets the prize? Run in such a way as to get the prize. Everyone who competes in the games goes into **strict training**. They do it to get a crown that will not last, but we do it to get a crown that will last forever."* 1 Corinthians 9:24-25

Principle #12 - PRAY! Talk to God

"Pray without ceasing." 1 Thessalonians 5:17 [KJV]

Definition: **pray** - a devout petition to God

I saved the most obvious principle for last. The word "pray" or "prayer" is just another way of saying "talking to God." You would think that Christians would have no problem with praying because talking to God should be the normal thing to do. From birth, children talk to their parents. They are inquisitive, observant, and they tend to do it naturally.

The same should be true in the relationship between a child of God and their Heavenly Father. Talking to God should come naturally as you build your personal relationship with Him.

You would be surprised to learn how many Christians shy away from prayer due to lack of knowledge or fear of approaching a Holy God. I believe this is a scheme of the enemy to prevent Christians from praying. He wants you to be too "scared" to approach God because he's hoping you will eventually give into that fear and stop praying. He wants to put it under the guise of "reverential" fear, but it's a lie from the pit of hell. God wants to hear from us every day. He is interested in what we have to say. He isn't sitting on His throne randomly selecting which prayers to listen to and which ones to reject. Prayers can be very eloquent and elaborate, or they can be short, sweet, and to the point. I'm not here to judge the quality or length of your prayer; my main concern is that you pray. The Bible clearly says that *"men ought always to pray, and not to faint"* (see Luke 18:1). Then why aren't we praying?

There are many reasons why people, even Christians, do not pray. One reason is that we often look to others for the solution instead of God. Why? Because it is human nature to reach out to another human being, our first point of contact tends to be our parent, spouse, or friend. Another reason is some people think that God is too busy orchestrating the world and doesn't have time for them. They often feel that they do not deserve to speak to God. Some people have a warped vision of God and compare Him with their natural father and feel since their natural father never cared about them, why would God? Lastly, some people just feel like they are the reason for being in a situation. It's their own fault, so why bother praying about it?

Whatever the reason for not making God your first point of contact during your struggles, you need to know He is the only one who can bring you out of your wilderness experience; therefore, talking to Him is KEY. He wants to be present to help in times of trouble, but you must believe that He cares for you, that He hears you, *"because anyone who comes to Him must believe that He exists and that He rewards those who earnestly seek Him."* (Hebrews 11:6) Keeping those communication lines open with God is crucial to hearing clear and specific directions to help direct you out of your unique situation.

But before you can listen to the Lord, you must break down any barrier that might hinder you from maintaining a strong and healthy relationship with Him. Below are a few ways to tear down those barriers:

1) **Clear the air** – God loves a contrite heart. We all fall short of the glory of God. But God in all His mercy always has a remedy—it's called "repentance." So take some time and quiet yourself before God and search your heart. Then let Him know that you've fallen short and ask His Forgiveness. This can take exactly two minutes or two hours, but whatever you do, don't get up from that place until you know that you have been forgiven. The enemy of your soul will try to block you on this, but you must believe the Word of God when it says, "whom the son has set free, he is free indeed." Use your sword—the Word of God—to confirm your forgiveness.

2) **Give thanks** – Once you have asked for forgiveness, thank God for His forgiveness and rejoice! You are clean and you are loved and there is nothing standing between you and your God.

3) **Share your heart** – Now that you are forgiven and have given thanks, continue talking to God. Let Him know what you are feeling; let Him know if you are hurting. Be brutally honest with Him. Don't hold back—He can handle anything you dish out.

While going through the wilderness, you might often feel alone. I shared in the chapter on isolation that you should not cut yourself off from the rest of the world. This is vital to understand because no man is an island, and it is God's divine will that we fellowship with one another. But all the fellowshipping in the world does not and should not take the place of communicating with the Lord.

Psalm 18:2 says, "**The LORD is my** rock, and my fortress, and my deliverer; my **God, my** strength, in whom I will trust; my **buckler**, and the horn of my salvation, and my high tower."

I like how the Living translations says it: "The Lord is my rock, my fortress, and my savior; my God is my rock, in whom I find protection. He is my shield, the power that saves me, and my place of safety."

No matter where you are, no matter what is going on in your life, no matter how you feel, you must ALWAYS believe that God is HERE for you! One of His redemptive names is Jehovah Shamma—"the Lord is there." He is an omnipresent God, which means He is everywhere at the same time. I know it may be a hard concept to comprehend, but that's what makes Him God. He has promised in His Word that He would never leave you or forsake you. He will never let you go. He loves you that much!

When I was going through my wilderness experience, I didn't talk to the Lord out loud like I used to. I "thought" my prayers, but I did not formally talk to Him at a specific time or place. I was used to talking to God all the time, but our relationship had become distant, and I did not like it. I knew I couldn't survive much longer without repairing my relationship with God. He could not use me in ministry if I wasn't seeking His direction. I couldn't experience His anointing if I wasn't staying in His face. I could not be an effective Christian if my communication lines with the Lord we're not fully restored. So, slowly I began to open up to Him again, and I started to share the deep feelings that I was experiencing in my heart.

I told Him I was lonely, that I was confused. I told Him that I did not like feeling separated from Him. I literally told Him every feeling I could possibly feel. And Praise God, He heard me! He began sending me the tools and weapons I needed in order to escape the wilderness.

As I stated earlier, a lot of people do not think that they can speak to God in such a manner. They think that their prayers need to be executed by dotting every "I" and crossing every "T," but sometimes you have to drop the formality and cry out, "Help, Lord!" and those two words will be just as effective as a two-hour prayer.

Talking to God is vital to your existence. The Bible declares that as we draw nigh to God, He will draw nigh to us. You are as close to God as **you** choose to be. Choose Him!

If you find yourself in the wilderness or a dry season of your life, keep those communication lines wide open. Talk to God all day long. That's what praying without ceasing really means: talking to God all day long. Keeping God first in your life. Keeping God forever on your mind. That's what keeps Him close to you, especially during those lonely seasons. God is waiting to hear from you. He's right there—and the ball is in your court.

Worshiping Through a Pandemic

*You will not fear the terror of night, nor the arrow that flies by day, nor the **pestilence** that stalks in the darkness, nor the **plague** that destroys at midday."*
Psalm 91:5-6 [NIV]

Definition: **pes·ti·lence** - any epidemic disease with a high death rate; a fatal epidemic disease
plague /plāg/ - a contagious bacterial disease characterized by fever and delirium

To be clear, not all wilderness experiences are self-induced. There are times that the Lord Himself may lead you through the wilderness for various reasons. The reasons can be as diverse as bringing you to a place of utter dependence on Him and building trust and faith, such as Much Afraid in the book *Hinds Feet in High Places*, mentioned in a previous chapter. Or it could be a time to develop humility such as when the children of Israel wandered in the wilderness for forty years.

Deuteronomy 8:2-3 gives a great explanation of why the Lord led Israel through the wilderness, but I see a pattern where this scripture can be also be true for His children today.

*"²Remember how the LORD your God led you all the way in the wilderness these forty years, to **humble and test** you in order to know*

*what was in your heart, whether or not you would keep His commands. ³ He humbled you, **causing you to hunger** and then feeding you with manna, which neither you nor your ancestors had known, **to teach you** that man does not live on bread alone but on every word that comes from the mouth of the LORD."*

We see in verses two and three where God clearly states His purposes:

1) To humble
2) To test
3) To cause hunger
4) To teach

Going through a wilderness experience in which you are having a hard time hearing God's voice is bad enough, but going through that same experience during a global pandemic is worse. Whether it be COVID, a political pandemic, or a racial pandemic, it's all designed to bring death to the nation.

As I stated before, we all go through seasons of drought in our lives. It could be spiritual as well as natural. For instance, you might be going through a season where you are at a standstill financially, or you may have a season of successful business ventures and then hit a plateau. Or maybe you're healthy as an ox, then get hit with all kinds of health challenges.

But imagine going through some of the roughest times of your life during a pandemic that leads to a national lockdown. That calls for a tremendous amount of self-discipline and dependency on the Lord.

In 2020, we were all hit with the COVID-19 pandemic. As a nation, we have not experienced anything as deadly or severe since the 1918 influenza pandemic. Nothing will cause fear, despair, and uncertainty like a killer you cannot see. To be honest, I don't know how anyone could go through something like this without having God in their lives. Thousands upon thousands of people lost their lives to this diabolical disease and everyone had to do their part just to stay alive. People had to practice social distancing, children had to use distant learning online, churches had to close their doors for a season, and restaurants had to become creative with takeout menus. We had to literally self-isolate and work from home, and at times that became unbearable for some. And God forbid that you contracted COVID to the point that it sent you to the hospital; I've been told that was the loneliest time a person could endure. Being separated from your loved ones for weeks, sometimes months in a lonely hospital room with no visitors except for a doctor or nurse who wore so much protective gear that you couldn't tell who they were; it had to be the ultimate rock bottom in anyone's life.

The common denominator was a lack of human contact. As I stated in my chapter on isolation, human beings were not built for isolation. In the prison system, they use isolation as a form of punishment, which can lead to all kinds of psychological, physical, and emotional problems in the inmates' lives. It is not God's design that we live a life of isolation, but in the midst of a pandemic, many were forced to.

But even then, God graciously gave us some avenues to maintain our sanity. FaceTime, Google Duo, and Zoom were only some options that allowed us to stay in touch by matching a face with a voice. But unfortunately, even that wasn't always enough to help people stay connected; many committed suicide because they still lacked that personal touch.

My pandemic experience was not as severe as most. I had to go into the office every day and I was able to shop with extreme caution, but not without my share of the loss of friends and family. I made it my business to stay connected to family and friends. I participated in weekly bible studies via Zoom, as well has staying connected with the intercessory team via text. I made sure not to isolate myself from the Body of Christ. But when I was going through my dry season, not feeling connected to the Lord, I had to work hard not to isolate myself from others. I needed to do life with someone else other than me, myself, and I.

As I said in a previous chapter, **worship is intentional**. So even if I was no longer in the physical building surrounded by physical people, I had to make the choice to worship God, right there in the privacy of my own four walls, just like I did when I was in a church service surrounded by hundreds of other believers.

It wasn't hard to worship because it's something I love to do, but it was definitely a challenge. I had to pull on my Vertical Worship principles once again to keep myself in check. I had to first repent to the Lord for being so lazy and lackadaisical—the exact thing I once accused the Body of Christ of being back in 2012.

I really desired to fellowship with Him with that same passion I experienced when I was first saved, but I got caught up with what I call the Romans 7:15 syndrome—*"for what I would, that do I not; but what I hate, that do I."*

There are tons of Christian messages and songs on YouTube and on Facebook to help me enter into worship, so I had no excuse. It was just that my get up and go, got up and left. The Lord had been so good to me. So fair, so dependable, so faithful. He had brought healing not only to myself, but to my elderly father that had both improved and extended our quality of life. He had met every one of my needs. He had sustained me. He had kept me—physically, emotionally, and mentally.

Yet, with all that knowledge and understanding, I still felt dry. Then I realized that He was doing all the giving and I was doing all the receiving. It was then when the Holy Spirit reminded me of Psalm 16:12-13; *"What shall I render to the Lord for all His goodness to me?"*

I had two choices; I could remain in the state of mind where I was, or I could get into the Word of God, turn to Colossians 3:1-3, and rehearse in my spirit what the Lord had spoken to me years before. I had to **seek** and **set** my affections on things above, and not on things on the earth. I had to meditate on these words and come into agreement with them again. It was only then that I got my groove back. Now I can worship the Lord vertically again.

Now I can worship the Lord vertically again. I had to pull on my Vertical Worship principles to keep myself in check. I had to first repent to the Lord for neglecting Him, then I had to get up and practice His presence, read the Word of God, sing love songs to the Lord, and maintain an open line of communication with Him through prayer. I had to allow the Holy Spirit to overshadow me so I could just bask in His presence once again. It was glorious!

There is a song that kept me grounded during the pandemic. It's called "In Over My Head" by Jenn Johnson of Bethel Music. Initially, you would think it's talking about getting into a situation that caused you to lose control because you were in too deep, but the Lord used this songwriter to take the words "in over my head" and turn them around to mean something completely different. When she sings about being "in over my head," she meant, "I'm getting deeper and deeper into the Lord, so much so that I am beautifully in over my head." This was masterful! I played this song over and over again because it signified where I was in that season of my life. And even though the pandemic has subsided a bit—stores are open, children are back in school, and churches have opened their doors—I still identify with the message of this song, and I think I always will.

In Over My Head (Crash Over Me)

I have come to this place in my life
I'm full but I've not satisfied
This longing to have more of You
And I can feel it my heart is convinced
I'm thirsty my soul can't be quenched
You already know this but still
Come and do whatever You want to

I'm standing knee deep
But I'm out where I've never been
I feel You coming
And I hear Your voice on the wind

Would You come and tear down the boxes
That I have tried to put You in
Let love come teach me who You are again
Would You take me back to the place
Where my heart was only about You
And all I wanted was just to be with You
Come and do whatever You want to

Further and further
My heart moves away from the shore
Whatever it looks like
Whatever may come I am Yours (2x)

Then You crash over me
And I've lost control but I'm free
I'm going under, I'm in over my head

And You crash over me
I'm where You want me to be
I'm going under, I'm in over my head

Whether I sink, whether I swim
Oh it makes no difference
When I'm beautifully in over my head

Whether I sink, whether I swim
It makes no difference
When I'm beautifully in over my head
And I am beautifully in over my head
Beautifully in over my head

In Over My Head (Crash Over Me) Song by Bethel Music, Jenn Johnson
We Will Not Be Shaken (Live) Album 2015

Worshiping through Sickness

You shall serve the Lord your God, and he will bless your bread and your water, and I will take **sickness** *away from among you.*
Exodus 23:25 [NIV]

Definition - **sick·ness** - the state of being ill.

Worshiping while you are sick is difficult. Lying in bed with pain shooting through your body, the last thing you feel like doing is talking—not even to God. Your mind is set on trying to get well. So, you lay there, listen to the doctor's report, and take your medicine. But there comes a point where you have to decide whose report you will believe—the doctor's or the Lord's. When you are sick, you may not have the strength to get out of bed, much less kneel or lay prostrate on the floor. You may not even have your voice; sometimes all you can do is slightly lift a hand.

But God is so good, because even though I wasn't giving Him the time He deserved, even though I wasn't going to church on a regular basis (largely due to the pandemic), He still met me where I was. Aren't you glad that God's movement in your life isn't contingent on what you do for Him, but on what He already did? He still saw fit to reveal Himself to me as Jehovah Rapha—the Lord that Heals—and His sovereignty shone through in two significant times in my life.

The first was in 2019 when my father was rapidly declining due to a condition called spinal stenosis. We didn't understand what was happening at first; all we knew was that he had once been a very active senior who could ride a bike, drive a car, mow his lawn, cook his own meals, and take care of his own home, and suddenly he began to lose his balance and fall constantly. He lost control of his hand movements and went from using a cane to a walker to a wheelchair in a matter of months.

It was a drastic change that took a toll on both of us, changing our lifestyles. I had to move back home because he could no longer live alone. I had to research and find home health aides and volunteers to help him get to doctor visits. He couldn't write and had to use a pencil to make a call on his cell phone. It got to the point where I had to help him in and out of bed, help him wash and put on his clothes. His paralysis was crippling him at a rapid pace, and according to his physical therapist, he was headed toward a bedridden future. He was miserable, but he was so strong. One night, I was helping him into bed and a tear quietly ran down his cheek. That nearly broke my heart, yet he never once complained.

In the meantime, I was operating on autopilot. I still went to church, still served in ministry, but I was very much perplexed and not sure of our future. I had the prayer warriors praying, but I was merely existing. Then, just as suddenly as this illness came upon my father, the Lord miraculously led us to the right place to begin his healing process.

The Lord used my father's faith to facilitate his own healing. He saw a commercial on television advertising a clinic that specialized in spinal conditions and simply told me he wanted to go. After his initial consultation, they advised a dangerous surgery with no guarantees; it could either stop the paralysis or make him worse. We consulted with my brothers and their wives on a three-way phone call, and we all agreed that if this was what he wanted to do, we would stand in agreement with him that the surgery would bring his deliverance. I thank God for praying brothers and sisters-in-law! He went on to have the surgery, and the paralysis was reversed. Within a matter of months, he went from a wheelchair to a walker to a cane and was back to his normal activities! Praise God! The Lord miraculously stepped in and proved Himself to be Jehovah Rapha.

The second time the Lord revealed Himself as my Healer was in the midst of the COVID-19 pandemic. In 2020, while thousands of people around me were dying from the disease, I was dying of sepsis and didn't even know it. But God, in His infinite mercy, said not so.

One Thursday morning, after walking a mile the day before, I woke up and could barely walk. I thought I had a slipped disk or my bladder had dropped because of the tremendous pressure I felt in my abdomen. I called in sick but quickly realized that I needed help, so I called my manager and asked him to come to my house to help me into my car. It took all the strength I had to muster up baby steps to walk down the steps with his help, and he literally had to put my legs in the car.

After a chiropractor's visit and a consultation with my doctor on the phone, I was advised that I should go to the hospital. My manager, seeing what bad shape I was in, advised me to call an ambulance. I told him I could drive; I just couldn't walk. So I drove myself to the hospital over 50 miles away.

On my way to the hospital, I developed a 103-degree fever. In the emergency room, the doctors detected blood in my urine and bacteria in my blood and I was later diagnosed as septic. I did not know what that meant exactly, but the nurse told me that I was a very sick young lady and gave me a printout of what sepsis was. *"A serious condition resulting from the presence of harmful microorganisms in the blood or other tissues, and the body's response to their presence can potentially lead to the malfunctioning of various organs, shock, and death."*

The enemy was trying to take me out, but God had a greater plan for me. I was in the hospital for five days. Once they got the infection under control, I was sent home with a pic line (I had to take antibiotics intravenously every day for a month) and on a walker.

When we arrived at my father's house, I could not even lift my legs high enough to walk up the steps. Neighbors had to take my Dad's old wheelchair out of the storage room and bump me up the steps backwards. Every move hurt. It hurt to stand, to turn, to sit, and it hurt to walk.

It took over three months of physical therapy to learn how to walk again, but God proved Himself to be Jehovah Rapha in my life, even when I didn't know I was sick, and I will forever be grateful to Him. He proved to me that even though I was clinging to life, both spiritually and physically, that He was still Lord over my life and the situation. It was the same sweet Holy Spirit I spoke about in my chapter on how I worshiped vertically in the wilderness, Who led me to go to the hospital just in time. For you see, I didn't go to the hospital because I had any symptoms of sepsis or a bad UTI, which was the initial cause of the sepsis. I went to the hospital because I couldn't walk, and after I arrived, they were able to diagnose the condition and treat the symptoms, sparing me from an untimely death. Our God is an awesome God!

And what was so strategic about this situation was the fact that He had just healed my father of a debilitating disease a year prior, only to become my primary caregiver! I had to move back in with him, and now he had to cook for me and give me my ice packs and medications. Our God has a sense of humor, doesn't He?

I will forever be grateful to the Lord for revealing Himself as not only Jehovah Rapha, the Lord my Healer; but also Jehovah Jireh, the Lord my Provider; and Jehovah Shalom, the Lord my Peace. Even in my driest season, God proved Himself to be Jehovah Shammah—the Lord is There—and He is always there, even when we aren't.

Worshiping Through Grief

"The Lord is near to the brokenhearted and saves the crushed in spirit."
Psalm 34:18 [NKJV]

Definition: **grief** - deep and poignant distress caused by or as if by bereavement

Losing a loved one can be the most devastating time in your life. There is a void left in your life that you feel can never be filled. Your closeness with the person you lost relates directly to the depth of your pain. You feel like a part of you died along with them. You can't focus, and you either can't eat or want to eat everything. You have to plan a funeral, write an obituary, and entertain guests. You operate on auto pilot because you have to. It is not until the funeral is over, the burial is done, and the people go back home that the rawness of your loss is magnified. Your emotions are all over the place. Some people cry and others hold it in. You have to begin to live in a "new normal"—a life without your loved one. And in the midst of all this, where is God?

Sometimes, people get mad at Him. "Where were You, God?" "You could have prevented this death." "You could have healed my mother." "Why did you take my child?" "I served You faithfully, and this is how You repay me?"

And that's okay. God can handle your anger. He sees your pain and He will be quietly waiting for you when you are ready to resume your relationship with Him.

Or you can respond like Martha, who questioned Jesus in John 11:21. "Lord," Martha said to Jesus, "if you had been here, my brother would not have died. But I know that even now God will give you whatever you ask."

We all respond to grief differently. There is no set of rules or how-to steps to get over it. You may never get over it, but you can learn to live through it. What works for me may not work for you. How I processed my grief may not be the way you processed yours.

Some of us can let go faster than others. Some people want to clean out their loved one's closet and give away anything that reminds them of their loss, whereas others cannot bring themselves to move anything. They can't even move their toothbrush out of the bathroom. I had a hard time saying the word "died." I would say my mother was gone, or she transitioned to heaven, but I could not say "my mother died" for years. I also had a hard time changing the name in my cell phone from Mom and Dad's house to Dad's house.

Any loss can either draw you closer to God or push you further from Him. The death of a loved one can be so devastating that even the strongest Christian can be knocked off their feet. It is a very sad season in your life, and it can be one of the loneliest seasons you will ever experience. You cannot rush the process. It's over when it's over, but you have to be careful not to get stuck in your grief.

Let me make this clear—you will never "get over" the loss of your loved one, but you will and can get through it. There will come a time when it won't hurt as much. There will come a time when you can think about them and smile instead of cry. When you can make it through their birthday and be okay. But it will take time. There will be triggers. You will see someone that reminds you of them, or you may smell the cologne they wore or food they cooked. There will be certain holidays that will trigger memories and a sense of loss. All of this is completely normal, and you cannot beat yourself up thinking you should be "over it."

It's hard to worship when you are hurting. It's hard to worship when you are sad. But what I love about God is that He is always there. You do not have to say a word, but know that He is right there with you. He is the silent partner in your grief. When He promised never to leave you or forsake you, He meant it. This is when He reveals Himself as Jehovah Shammah—the Lord is There. And He is ready to comfort you as much as you will allow Him to.

When my mother was dying of cancer, I had the privilege to stay with her till the end. Every morning, I got up around 6 am and went for a walk to clear my head. I used that time to talk to God, pray, sing, and worship. I knew that what my mother was going through was more than I could physically handle, so I pulled on my relationship with God. We believed in God for a miracle. We believed in God for complete healing and restoration. I started to help build my mom's faith by reading her scriptures on healing, showing videos of people who were miraculously healed of cancer, and for a while, it looked like it was working. My mom got stronger, and even the hospice Chaplin noticed the difference, but we later learned that it was just a surge of terminal lucidity she experienced before she finally passed away. Although it gave me false hope, I was grateful for that surge. It gave us time. Time to grow closer to each other and, more importantly, to God.

During this season, I wasn't overly demonstrative in my worship. I wasn't going around speaking in tongues, but I was silently staying connected with the Lord. I kept Him close. He was my anchor. He gave me the strength to watch my mother take her last breath, call hospice, call my brother, and send my father into the room to say his final goodbye.

I wrote her obituary and even gave an altar call at her funeral, but that didn't mean I was okay. I was coasting on the strength and grace of God. Psalm 34:18 says, "The Lord is near to the brokenhearted and saves the crushed in spirit." And I found that to be very true.

And even though I had God to lean on, I also had the help of a support group. There are a lot of mixed opinions about support groups, but I truly believe the Lord's hand was still in the midst of the support group. There are many wonderful grief support groups available to meet you where you are, but the one I used is called GriefShare, which is Christian-based and nationwide. They set up support groups in churches all over the country designed to walk through the grieving process with you.

Living through grief is a form of living in the wilderness. It's dark, it's dry, and it's lonely. But I praise God for giving us the tools to get through this dark period of our lives. When He gave us the promise of the comfort of the Holy Spirit, He had grief in mind.

Our God feels. Our God is compassionate, and our God grieves. And I have to believe that this big omniscient God that I keep bragging about is in control.

Coming Out of the Fog...I Choose Christ

"I'm energized every time I enter Your heavenly sanctuary to seek more of your power and drink in more of Your glory."
Psalm 63:2 [TPT]

Definition: **fog** - something that obscures and confuses a situation or someone's thought processes

God would not lead you into the wilderness and leave you there. With every wilderness experience and dry season, He has already provided a remedy to lead you out of it.

The Lord has a plan and purpose for your life and that doesn't include you remaining in a desolate place for the rest of your life.

Even while in the wilderness, you are still God's representative. People are still watching how you respond in the darkest times in your life as well as the victorious ones. Your response is key. It can either inspire and encourage or it can turn off and discourage others.

I'm not saying that you have to walk around with a fake smile plastered on your face 24/7. It's okay for people to see your struggle. It's okay for them to see your tears and even your frustration, because when God brings you out of your wilderness, what a glorious testimony it will be for others to witness your strength and tenacity and utter dependence on God.

So whether you gracefully walk out of the wilderness or have to crawl to the finish line, just know that there IS a finish line. Weeping may endure for a night, but joy comes in the morning. And even though we do not know how long the night we have to endure will last, press through to the time of rejoicing that is promised to come in the morning.

Hebrews 12:2 speaks of Jesus when He was about to go to the cross on our behalf. For the JOY set before Him, He endured the cross despite the shame and is now sitting on the throne at the right hand of God. Jesus and all that the Kingdom of God represents is the JOY waiting for us. Despite the shame of going through the wilderness experience, we can ENJOY the FULLNESS of our God as He continues to navigate us through this thing called life until He finally calls us home.

I knew I was coming out of the wilderness because there was a definite shift in the atmosphere for me. That spiritual sluggishness had lifted. The Lord was opening doors for me, and I began to walk through them. I took advantage of the opportunities He was laying before me.

I knew the fog was lifting when I started getting up early every day to meet with God. This is something I had been longing to do for years, but I was always "too tired" to get up and get down on my knees, and now I was doing it effortlessly.

I knew I was coming out of the fog when I started hungering and thirsting for more of God. I was getting back into my Bible and treating it like that love letter I always knew it to be.

Another indicator that the fog was lifting was my job. I had been seeking new employment for years, and it seemed like the heavens were brass. I have always treated my jobs as assignments from God. There was always someone there whom He wanted me to minister to, or simply just to live a godly life in front of them so they could observe a Christ-centered life modeled before them. So I knew this door was one that only the Lord could open.

For years, I asked when my assignment would be over, and for years He would say, "not now," or nothing at all, which was the equivalent of "not now." I was miserable and wanted out; I felt like this job was my personal wilderness and I was struggling to get out of it. But suddenly He opened not one but multiple doors to new employment, and I was finally blessed with the job of my dreams.

Lastly, I knew I was coming out of the fog when He led me to my current church and I started reconnecting with the Body of Christ on a deeper level. My soul was coming alive again, and a fresh anointing had come over me.

I love to pray for others, so one of the first ministries I joined was the intercessory prayer team. It was funny to me how in the past I had loved to intercede for others, but now, it was like I had to learn how to pray all over again. I could tell that the intimacy I once had wasn't quite there like before, and it was like I had to retrain myself by praying for others. It was a little awkward at first, but I stayed with it until I got back into position with God again and allowed the Holy Spirit to pray through me.

I also had to get back on track with my tithing. Tithing was something I always loved to do, but I did have a slight fear of the lack of funds. Then one Sunday, Pastor Jud taught on the principle of tithing in a way that I had never heard before, and it released me to want to go out and tithe off any income that came across my path. He shared how tithing was not about the money but about stewardship and being obedient to God, and how we had to replace the fear of not having enough with faith that God would take care of us.

When I came to the realization that it was God's money and I was only a steward, and the fact He had already claimed His 10%, it was easier to let go. Once again, a sudden influx of money came into my life between the old job and the new and tax rebates, and I was overjoyed to be able to practice the principle of tithing and be obedient to God. Hallelujah—I could finally see the light at the end of the tunnel!

I once read that when the children of Israel left Egypt, their trip from the wilderness to the promised land only should have taken between 11 and 40 days, but because of their disobedience, murmuring, and complaining, it took 40 years. There were times when the Lord performed miracles and they rejoiced, but because of the mundane routine, they found themselves right back where they had been before. Yes, it is a vicious cycle to break. But the good news is that it can be broken!

It's a matter of choice. I could either pack up all my doubt, discouragement, and fears and throw them in my wilderness luggage and walk into my newfound freedom, or I could stay in the wilderness for another 40 years and be miserable and isolated.

I chose the former.

While in the wilderness, I had to make some serious decisions. Before I could walk all the way out of the wilderness, I had to choose to do a few things first that would serve the devil my eviction notice. Below are my declarations:

- ❖ I chose to hold on to God even in the midst of a drought.

- ❖ I chose to worship God even if it was only for a few minutes a day.

- ❖ I chose to acknowledge the deity of God and practice His presence even if I didn't feel it.

- ❖ I chose to tell God that I loved Him because I knew He loved me, and this too shall pass.

- ❖ I chose to lift up God's name and make declarations of His character.

- ❖ I chose to stop wandering in the wilderness.

Once out of the wilderness, I had to make declarations as I moved into my new address:

- ❖ I choose to turn my face upward toward God.

- ❖ I choose to make time for God.

- ❖ I choose to put God above every other god in my life, including the TV, cell phone, computer, and my job.

- ❖ I choose to sit with God and enjoy His Presence.

- ❖ I choose to share God's goodness with others and share how much He loves them and can bring them out of their wilderness experiences.

Our relationship with God is different from any other relationship we will ever have. It's the only relationship we have where the other person is invisible. In all our other relationships, we are dealing with human beings in the flesh. With God, it is 100% by faith. It's unique in the fact that although we cannot touch, feel, or even see Him in the natural world, we can experience the fullness of His Presence in the Spirit.

Being in His presence brings clarity. Creativity begins to flow. Ideas and concepts are formed. Therefore, we must learn how to tap into our spiritual side and live there. We must abide in the spirit and give no place to our flesh. Now I don't mean that we have to be so heavenly minded that we are no longer earthly good, nor am I suggesting that we go around floating on a cloud with a halo and harp. But let us live our daily lives with purpose by being intentional about living a Spirit-filled life.

When we share our feelings with others, whether it be our parents, children, spouses, or co-workers, it's either in person, by phone, or through a letter or social media. Then they in turn respond with either words of affirmation, agreement, passion, or anger and even hate. But with the Lord, it's different. Our relationship was initially built on words of repentance and acceptance, and we eventually moved on to words of passion and love.

When we sing songs like:

- "You Are the Air I Breathe"
- "I Surrender"
- "He Touched Me"
- "When I Look Into Your Holiness - Gaze Upon Your Loveliness"

We are trying to relate to God through our senses, because that's all we have. We may not be able to see God, but we can surely feel His Presence. We know by the Spirit that He is in the room. Consequently, we know when He is grieved and has left the room. It's a spiritual thing.

God is Spirit, and those who worship Him must worship Him in Spirit and Truth. As humans, we are body, soul, and spirit, but it's with our spirit that we commune with God. Therefore, we must maintain a healthy spiritual life.

There is so much going on in the world today, and we can easily be swayed away from the things of God and push God right out of our lives. Hence the acronym was born: EGO—Easing God Out. The Word of God admonishes us in Ephesians 6:10-18 to put on the full armor of God, because the Lord knew that as Christians, we would be in a continuous spiritual fight for our sanity, healing, deliverance, and prosperity. We know our struggle is not against flesh and blood, but against the rulers, the authorities, the powers of this dark world, and against the spiritual forces of evil in the heavenly realms. We cannot afford to lay down our swords (the Word of God) and take a spiritual siesta!

So, what can we do to maintain this loving relationship with God? How can we stay consistent in this fast-paced culture? DETERMINATION! Here are ten tips to cultivate your relationship with the Lord:

1) **Confess** your commitment to God.

2) **Talk to Him every day.** It doesn't have to be formal. He is your Father and He longs to hear from you, whether you are sitting, standing, or lying down.

3) **Don't shut Him out!** Share everything with Him—the good, the bad, and the ugly. He knows it all anyway; He's just waiting for you to be transparent with Him and invite Him into your world.

4) **Get your daily heart check-up.**

"I the LORD search the heart and test the mind, to give every man according to his ways, according to the fruit of his deeds." Jeremiah 17:10 (ESV)

"Keep your heart with all vigilance, for from it flow the springs of life." Proverbs 4:23 (ESV)

"And I will give you a new heart, and a new spirit I will put within you. And I will remove the heart of stone from your flesh and give you a heart of flesh." Ezekiel 36:26 (ESV)

5) **Let your heart be a resting place for His Presence.** Let your heart be an inviting place for Him to dwell.

6) **Be brutally honest with Him.** According to Psalm 139, He knows your thoughts afar off.

7) **Don't be ruled by your emotions.** Galatians 5:16 says, "But I say, walk by the Spirit, and you will not gratify the desires of the flesh."

8) **Learn to laugh with Him.** Invite Him into the quirky side of yourself.

9) **Keep the spark alive!** Let the joy of the Lord truly be your strength.

10) **Be Intentional.** When it all boils down to it, it's a matter of choice.

- ❖ You must choose to walk in the Spirit.

- ❖ You must choose to talk to God every day.

- ❖ You must choose to read the Bible every day.

- ❖ You must choose to include Him in every aspect of your life.

- ❖ You must choose to love Him.

- ❖ You must choose to worship Him.

- ❖ You must choose to get out of your despair and seek Him out.

The Benefits of Worshiping in the Wilderness

"O God of my life, I'm lovesick for you in this weary wilderness. I thirst with the deepest longings to love you more, with cravings in my heart that can't be described... Daily I will worship you passionately and with all my heart."
Psalm 63:1&4 [TPT]

Definition: **ben·e·fit** - an advantage or profit gained from something

Whether you are in a dry season or going through a pandemic, sickness, or grief, what you are feeling is very real. Do not let anyone tell you to **'get over it'** because it is not that simple.

I can say beyond a shadow of a doubt that worshiping vertically was the thing that helped me get through this dry spell. Keeping Him first in my thoughts, surrounding myself with worship music, listening to the Word when I couldn't read it, surrounding myself with other believers of like mind, and talking to the Lord daily even when it wasn't in a formal prayer time were all the "natural" things I did because I had already experienced years of walking closely with the Lord. It was in my bones.

Some people say that you should fake it till you make it. That is, keep doing a thing until you begin to really believe it. All I know is that you must have a "want to" spirit. You must want to serve God, to love God and be close to God, if you will have any success getting through your dry season. There is nothing you can do to "earn" His love or to get back into His good graces, because you already have His love from way back on calvary. You cannot do anything to earn it or deserve it, but what you can do is pray and ask the Lord to ignite His fire once again in you. You can dust off your Bible and begin to read again about the nature of God. You can talk to Him from a contrite heart and be completely honest with Him about where you are in your walk with Him and how much you love Him.

I learned a lot during my wilderness experience. God has a way of helping you learn life lessons through your life experiences. As the old saying goes, "it's not what happened to you that matters, it's what **you do** about what happened to you." Your response to the hard things in life is critical if you are going to grow into a mature Christian. A lot of these changes will happen in the inner workings of your heart. It's not for all to see. Psalm 51:6 says, "Behold, thou desirest truth in the inward **parts**; And **in the hidden part** thou wilt make me to know wisdom." I love this scripture because it makes the experience that much more intimate—something between you and the Lord. Going through difficult times will either make you or break you. If you allow the process to run its course, you will come out of the wilderness with so many valuable truths to share with those who are in the beginning stages of their own wilderness experiences. And hopefully it will give them the extra push to make it to the other side.

Here are some things I have learned:
1) Worshiping God does not always come freely, even to the more seasoned worshiper. It takes initiative and tenacity.
2) I learned how to solely depend on the Holy Spirit.
3) Dying to self isn't as easy as I thought it would be. It takes perseverance and determination to die to self and come alive to Christ. It doesn't happen overnight; it is a daily process, so take it day by day.
4) I learned how to delight myself in the Lord. Find the things that bring Him joy. Seek ways to let Him know how wonderful He is to me.
5) It is absolutely necessary to digest the Word of God every day.
6) I learned that I was in the fight of my life. I could have easily backslidden or given into my carnality, which would have resulted in me being less effective for the Kingdom.
7) I learned that I had to seek and set my affections on things above and not on those things in the world.
8) Practicing God's Presence is being fully aware of His Presence everywhere you go realizing that He is Omnipresent.

Just because you are going through a dry season doesn't mean that you have to leave God out of your season. The Bible says in Proverbs 3:6 that we are to acknowledge Him in all our ways and **He will direct our path**. That means He will direct our paths in the on-fire times of our lives as well as the lukewarm times. He wants to be actively involved in everything we do, wherever we are in life. It is a balancing act, going through a stage in your life when you don't want to pray, study, or minister, yet you don't want to let go of God either. This is the time to stay closer to Him than ever before. Just because you are going through a wilderness experience doesn't mean you are not still a child of God. It just means that you are a child of God going through a wilderness experience.

The concept of Vertical Worship has been a lifeline for me. It helped me maintain my sanity. It helped me keep my priorities in order: God first, everything else second (I even put this on a T-shirt). It helped me desire to demonstrate my love of God to the rest of the world. To seek out ways to show my adoration to Jesus Christ.

Louis Giglio once said, "My worship is singular." Singular means to be single-minded. One purpose in mind. I don't know about you, but my mind is so cluttered with things—life, my job, and an array of emotions—that it often takes me an hour just to de-clutter my mind and focus on the Lord. But learning to direct my worship vertically has kept me connected to the Lord, even in the midst of my busyness.

Our personal relationship with God is crucial to the success of any other relationship we have here on the earth. Therefore, while I do recognize the importance of horizontal relationships with mankind, our unique calling is to put emphasis on our vertical relationship with the Lord.

Vertical Worship is essential to maintaining a real relationship with the Lord, no matter what you are going through. God's gifts are given without repentance, and while He still loves us in the midst of our sin, there is a significant difference between being used by God while you are in a compromising position as opposed to being used by God while in a totally surrendered position.

I Promise You

"You, who have shown me great and severe troubles, shall revive me again, and bring me up again from the depths of the earth. You shall increase my greatness, and comfort me on every side"

Psalm 71:20-21 [Amplified]

Definition: **prom·ise** - a declaration or assurance that one will do a particular thing or that a particular thing will happen

We experience a lot of valleys as Christians, and to be honest with you, it's not the low times in our lives that knock us out of whack as much as the normal times. The mundane nature of life, doing the same thing day in and day out, lacking excitement. It's the same old same old things, the boredom of life that causes us to dive into reality TV, into other people's lives, just to get our minds off of our own mundane lives—well, at least that was my truth. This can easily cause a spiritual drought.

We must break the vicious cycle. But to be honest, sometimes we are just too tired, weak, or downright lazy to fight back. So instead, we give in and find ourselves wandering in the wilderness for years.

I have been saved for more than 40 years. I have been on the mountain top, in the valley, and everywhere in between, and there are several things I have learned after all these years. I've learned that there are various dimensions to your walk with the Lord. You won't always wake up singing His praises. You won't always make the right decisions. But one thing I can attest to is this: if your heart is in the right place, He will hear you. If, through all your craziness, you don't become a complete fool and turn your back on Him, He will still talk to you. He will still guide you, as much as you let Him, along the way. He is still a Merciful God.

I've been there, done that, got the T-shirt and am currently recording the video, and one thing remains the same—God is in control of every phase of my life. I can do nothing without Him, and because of Him, I am a survivor.

If you take hold of the principles and scriptures shared in this book and allow the Holy Spirit to have a chief place in your life, I promise you the following things will begin to manifest in your life:

- ❖ Your love relationship with the Lord will grow.

- ❖ Your peace will be restored.

- ❖ Your spiritual health will be restored and refreshed time and time again.

- ❖ A new sense of courage and strength will emerge from the ashes.

- ❖ Your passion will begin to ignite, even when the embers grow dim.

- ❖ Your confidence in God, who He is and how much He loves you, will grow deeper roots.

"You are such a rich banquet of pleasure to my soul. I lie awake each night thinking of You and reflecting on how You help me like a father. I sing through the night under Your splendor-shadow, offering up to You my songs of delight and joy! With passion I pursue and cling to You. Because I feel Your grip on my life, I keep my soul close to Your heart." Psalm 63:7-8 (TPT)

The End

Let My Life Be Worship

This moment is holy and I hear You calling
I turn my face towards You and my heart is open
You're always pursuing and my life's surrendered
You have my affection
So let my life be worship
And let my heart stay true
May my love never grow cold
May it burn forevermore
May my life be worship to You, oh
In blessing, in sorrow, in the ordinary
Whatever the cost is, You're always worthy
My heart's cry and my whole life is for Your glory
You have my attention
So let my life be worship
Let my heart stay true
May my love never grow cold
May it burn forevermore
Let my life be worship to You, oh
So let it be, let it be worship
You're the only one, only one worth it
Nothing is like You, there's no one beside You
Only You're worthy, You're worthy

So let it be, let it be worship

You're the only one, only one worth it

Nothing is like You, there's no one beside You

Only You're worthy, You're worthy

So let it be, let it be worship

You're the only one, only one worth it

Nothing is like You, there's no one beside You

Only You're worthy, You're worthy

So let my life be worship

Let my heart stay true

So let my life be worship

Let my heart stay true

May my love never grow cold

May it burn forevermore

Let my life be worship to You

In everything, in everything

Let My Life Be Worship lyrics © Bethel Music Publishing,
Songwriters: Jess Clayton Cates / Jenn Johnson / Sam Hart / Michaela Gentile
Bethel Worship Publishing, Brian And Jenn Publishing

REFERENCES

Benefits definition - Google Search. (n.d.).

https://www.google.com/search?q=benefits+definition

Bethesda Senior Living. (2018, October 09). *3 reasons why we go through spiritually dry seasons.* Bethesda Senior Living Communities. https://www.bethesdaseniorliving.com/blog/3-bible-verses-for-seasons-of-change

Definition of acknowledge. (2023). In *Merriam-Webster Dictionary.* https://www.merriam-webster.com/dictionary/acknowledge

Definition of beginning. (2023). In *Merriam-Webster Dictionary.*

https://www.merriam-webster.com/dictionary/beginning

Definition of change. (2023). In *Merriam-Webster Dictionary.*

https://www.merriam-webster.com/dictionary/change

Definition of dance. (2023). In *Merriam-Webster Dictionary.*

https://www.merriam-webster.com/dictionary/dance

Definition of deity. (2023). In *Merriam-Webster Dictionary.*

https://www.merriam-webster.com/dictionary/deity

Definition of epiphany. (2023). In *Merriam-Webster Dictionary.*

https://www.merriam-webster.com/dictionary/epiphany

Definition of grief. (2023). In *Merriam-Webster Dictionary.*

https://www.merriam-webster.com/dictionary/grief

Definition of know. (2023). In *Merriam-Webster Dictionary.*

https://www.merriam-webster.com/dictionary/know

Definition of love. (2023). In *Merriam-Webster Dictionary*.
https://www.merriam-webster.com/dictionary/love

Definition of new. (2023). In *Merriam-Webster Dictionary*.
https://www.merriam-webster.com/dictionary/new

Definition of season. (2023). In *Merriam-Webster Dictionary*.
https://www.merriam-webster.com/dictionary/season

Definition of uncultivated. (2023). In *Merriam-Webster Dictionary*.
https://www.merriam-webster.com/dictionary/uncultivated

Definition of vertical. (2023). In *Merriam-Webster Dictionary*.
https://www.merriam-webster.com/dictionary/vertical

Definition of wilderness. (2023). In *Merriam-Webster Dictionary*.
https://www.merriam-webster.com/dictionary/wilderness

Definition of worship. (2023). In *Merriam-Webster Dictionary*.
https://www.merriam-webster.com/dictionary/worship

DeShazzo, L. (1982). Lord, You are more precious than silver [Hymn]. On *9 hymnals*, Integrity's Hosanna! Music.

Dictionary.com. (n.d.). *Home*. https://www.dictionary.com/

Donne, J. (n.d.). *No Man is an Island.* The Idioms.
https://www.theidioms.com/no-man-is-an-island/

Drought definition - Google Search. (n.d.).
https://www.google.com/search?q=drought+definition

Easton, M. G. (2015). *Easton's Bible dictionary.* CreateSpace Independent Publishing Platform

Exercise definition - Google Search. (n.d.).
https://www.google.com/search?q=exercise+definition

Fog definition - Google Search. (n.d.).

https://www.google.com/search?q=fog+definition

Friend. (n.d.). In *TheFreeDictionary.com.*

https://www.thefreedictionary.com/friend

Fry, S. L. (2001). Oh the Glory of Your Presence- lyrics [Song]. On *Songs 4 Worship: Be Glorified*, Capitol CMG Publishing.

Gentile, M., Cates, J., Hart, S., & Johnson, J. (2021). Let My Life Be Worship-Lyrics [Song]. Bethel Music Publishing

Got Questions. (2022, January 4). *What does it mean to backslide?* GotQuestions.org.

https://www.gotquestions.org/backslide.html

Harris, L., McHugh, P., & Culross, D. (1987). *I Miss My Time with You.* Paragon.

Hurnard, H. (2017, November 7). *Hinds' Feet on High Places.* Tyndale House Publishers, Inc..

Isolate definition - Google Search. (n.d.).

https://www.google.com/search?q=isolate+definition

Johnson, J. (2019, May 14). *How long you can live without water.* Medical News Today.

https://www.medicalnewstoday.com/articles/325174%23summary

Johnson, J. L., & Gentile, J-P. (2014). In Over My Head (Crash Over Me)- Lyrics [Song]. On *We will not be shaken*, Bethel Music Publishing.

King James Bible online. (2023).
https://www.kingjamesbibleonline.org/

Klein, L. B. (1978). I Love You Lord-Lyrics [Song]. On *The Hymnal for Worship and Celebration.* CMG Publishing.

LeBlanc, L. (2013). There Is None Like You - Lyrics [Recorded by Don Moen and Paul Wilbur]. *Heal Our Land Album,* Integrity Music Song

Lucey, C. (2021). What does it mean to 'Set Your Mind on Things Above'? (Colossians 3:2). *Christianity.com.* https://www.christianity.com/wiki/heaven-and-hell/what-does-it-mean-to-set-your-mind-on-things-above.html

McAllen, P. (2014). Die to Myself – Lyrics [Song]. *I Hear Your Voice,* Pete McAllen

McManus, M. R. (2023). How solitary confinement works. *HowStuffWorks.* https://people.howstuffworks.com/solitary-confinement.htm

Mysteries of the Anointing Quotes by Benny Hinn. (n.d.). https://www.goodreads.com/work/quotes/92180726-mysteries-of-the-anointing

Nelson, T. (2015). *Sovereignty - Easton s Bible dictionary online.* biblestudytools.com. https://www.biblestudytools.com/dictionaries/eastons-bible-dictionary/sovereignty.html

Pastor, J. R. B. (2019, November 16). *US surgeons say pig kidney functional in human for more than a month* [Video]. Hickory

Daily Record. https://hickoryrecord.com/news/faith-and-values/meditation-how-can-we-survive-the-spiritual-wilderness/article_baabb576-6929-5648-b838-e657ebd4b56d.html

Paul, I. (2019, September 17). *What is 'the Word of God'?*. https://www.psephizo.com/

Pfeiffer, C. F. (1970). *Wycliffe Bible Encyclopedia*. Moody Publishers.

Plague definition - Google Search. (n.d.). https://www.google.com/search?q=plague+definition

Presence definition - Google Search. (n.d.). https://www.google.com/search?q=presence+definition

Principle definition - Google Search. (n.d.). https://www.google.com/search?q=principle+definition

Promise definition - Google Search. (n.d.). https://www.google.com/search?q=promise+definition

Prosch, K., & Davis, T. (n.d.). So Come Lyrics [Recorded by Israel Houghton]. Integrity Music.

Random House, Inc. (2012). *Pray definition & meaning*. Dictionary.com. https://www.dictionary.com/browse/pray

Reckless Love lyrics. (n.d.). [Recorded by Cory Asbury]. *Be Essential Songs*, Bethel Music Publishing.

Rolston, H. (2019). Midbar, arabah and eremos–Biblical Wilderness. *Environment and Society Portal*.

https://www.environmentandsociety.org/exhibitions/wilderness-babel/midbar-arabah-and-eremos-biblical-wilderness

Self definition - Google Search. (n.d.).

https://www.google.com/search?q=self+definition

Seth Yates Music. (2010). Holy- Lyrics [Song by Jesus Culture]. On *Consumed*, Watershed Worship Publishing.

Sickness definition - Google Search. (n.d.).

https://www.google.com/search?q=sickness+definition

Sing definition - Google Search. (n.d.).

https://www.google.com/search?q=sing+definition

Taylor, J. (2016, September 21). 'The Religious Affections' by Jonathan Edwards: A Q&A on an Evangelical Classic. *The Gospel Coalition.* https://www.thegospelcoalition.org/blogs/evangelical-history/the-religious-affections-by-jonathan-edwards-a-qa-on-an-evangelical-classic/

The Mayo Clinic Staff. (2017, September 27). Depression and anxiety: Exercise eases symptoms. *Mayo Clinic.* https://www.mayoclinic.org/diseases-conditions/depression/in-depth/depression-and-exercise/art-20046495

Tucker, D., Jr. (2014, June 5). *Remembering God's gift of water.* Duke. https://sites.duke.edu/theconnection/2014/06/05/

User, S. (2023, May 28). The Difference Between Happiness And Joy - Shop. *Shop.* https://positivelyjane.net/blog/difference-between-happiness-and-joy/

Walker, H. (2002) *I Need You to Survive* – Lyrics [Song] Hezekiah Walker & LFC – Family Affair II Life at Radio City Music Hall Album Published by Verity Records

Walker-Smith, K. (2012) "Holy Spirit" [Song] Lyrics. Jesus Culture (feat. Kim Walker-Smith) –Capitol Christian Music Group Publishing.

Wikipedia contributors. (2023). *Dry season.* Wikipedia. https://en.wikipedia.org/wiki/Dry_season

Wikipedia friendship - Google Search. (n.d.). https://www.google.com/search?q=Wikipedia+Friendship

YourDictionary. (n.d.). *Home: Definitions and meanings from over a dozen trusted dictionary sources.* https://www.yourdictionary.com/

Printed in the USA
CPSIA information can be obtained
at www.ICGtesting.com
JSHW050334011023
49303JS00004B/19

9 781088 282946